ODD PEOPLE: ANDAPU OYATE

ODD PEOPLE: ANDAPU OYATE

Friendships and Feuds between Pioneers and Native Americans

Shirley Bahlmann

Bonneville Books
Springville, Utah

ISBN: 1-55517-835-9
v.1

Published by Bonneville Books
an imprint of Cedar Fort, Inc.
925 N. Main Springville, Utah., 84663
www.cedarfort.com

Distributed by:

CEDAR FORT

Cover design by Nicole Williams
Cover design © 2005 by Lyle Mortimer

Printed in the United States of America
10 9 8 7 6 5 4 3 2 1

Printed on acid-free paper

Dedication

For my brother DellRay, aka Chief Spotted Horse, with whom I had the wonderful adventure of being named co-honorary member of the Ogallala Sioux Indian Tribe in the 1960s.

Contents

Preface

I was only about ten years old when I was granted honorary membership in the Sioux Indian tribe in Ogallala, Nebraska. This was high adventure for a New Jersey girl who was on her way to visit her grandparents in Utah and stopped with her family one evening to see an Indian performance.

At the end of the show, all the children in the audience were invited up on stage to dance with the Indians. I felt rather clumsy since I'd never danced an Indian dance before, and when the Indian chief sitting at the side of the stage motioned for me to come over to him, I had the unsettling feeling that I had somehow gotten myself into trouble. I thought that he was going to make me sign up for a class—Indian dance 101—that would take up all my summer vacation and maybe even prevent me from visiting my grandparents. When the drums stopped, however, the chief announced that I was now an honorary member of the tribe, and I was given the Indian name of Princess Roan Eagle.

What made the event even better is that my brother Dell-Ray was inducted into the tribe at the same time. He was given the name of Chief Spotted Horse. We were both crowned with Indian headdresses, and the chief asked us if we were twins. "No, sorry," I said. "We just look a lot alike and happen to be about the same height."

In later years, my brother and I have had several discussions about our adventure. We have come to wonder, tongue in cheek, how many blonde Princess Roan Eagles and Chief Spotted Horses there might be running around the United States of America.

Regardless of how many others may share my adopted name,

being selected as an Indian princess had a profound effect on me. Whenever I remember that evening, my heart lifts and my imagination stirs. What if my ancestors, instead of coming from Scandinavia and crossing the plains of the American West, had been on the other side, watching the blond, blue-eyed palefaces come into their ancestral land to settle in ever-increasing numbers?

In this collection of stories, I have done my best to portray the possible differences in the feelings of the Native Americans and pioneers. I have assumed that the written and oral accounts I have used in compiling these stories are true. There cover a variety of experiences that demonstrate some of the trials and triumphs of disparate cultures trying to coexist. As you will see, sometimes things went well, and sometimes they did not. Often, there was not a right side or wrong side—just different views.

It is not my intention to take sides. As strange as the whites may have found the Native Americans, I have to believe that the Indians found the appearance and beliefs of the pale-faced and light-eyed newcomers to be just as strange. Don't pass judgment unless you've walked a while in someone else's moccasins or high-buttoned shoes.

"Andapu Oyate" is Shoshone for "Odd People." It seemed fitting to give voice to both the Indians and the whites in a book that shows both points of view.

I have made every effort to portray the events herein as accurately as possible within the framework of first-person narrative, adding details that I felt would enhance the story and convey its message with maximum impact. I used various historical documents, various family histories, out-of-print books, and oral accounts to compile this collection of stories. It is my wish that all who read these accounts, whether they're familiar with the stories or not, will find value in them and use the life lessons they teach to better their own lives and the lives of others.

There is evidence from treaties, Indian reservation records, and baptismal documents that the dominant Indian tribe inhabiting Utah at the time the pioneers arrived in 1847 was not Ute but Shoshone. When Indian reservations were first established, records list seven bands of Ute Indians assigned to reservations in Colorado. In the meantime, Shoshones were being adopted and baptized by Mormon families in Utah. It wasn't until the late 1800s that the Colorado Utes were moved onto northern and southern Utah Territory reservations. Some past historians have mistakenly identified all Indians within Utah's boundaries as Utes. In fact, there were small traveling bands of Utes, Navajo, and Paiutes, among others, but the evidence indicates that Chief Walker (Wakara), Aropeen, Black Hawk, Tabiona, and many others written of in the annals of Utah history were Shoshone.

Acknowledgments

A big thanks to Mike Kohut for his help with research.

Thanks to Mike Lynes for taking the time to answer my questions on pioneer dwellings at Winter Quarters.

Thank you, Arthella Larsen, for keeping me informed, and thanks to Doyle for keeping Michael busy!

A special thanks to my triplet nieces, Jessica, Jennifer, and Jacquelyn McGarry, for chasing down my manuscript pages when they tipped out of my bag and blew across the Manti Temple Hill, and thanks also to various Mormon Miracle Pageant cast members who helped gather up the errant pages.

Thanks to Jeanie Lloyd for her expert information on horses.

Thanks to Shauna Wayman for her cheerful babysitting service.

As always, thanks to my proofreaders who make my books worth reading: Val Sorensen, Jennie Mickelson, Judi Hansen, Laurie Allen, and Bob Bahlmann

Thanks to Sharon Kay Anderson for cluing me in on some great Internet research sites and sharing some family stories with me.

Thank you, Linnie Findlay, for research help on American Indians.

And thanks to my Father in Heaven for giving me the gift of writing. It's a blast!

Remember Me?

"I have a bad feeling about this," Abe said.

I turned to him, my surprise showing plainly on my face. "Why? We said our prayers this morning."

Abe shook his head. "If you pray for safety and then jump off the ship into the ocean to take a swim, do you deserve to be saved from drowning?"

I smiled. Maybe I didn't share my companion's gloomy outlook because I'd had enough experiences in the past fifty years to make me feel confident throwing my lot in with the Lord's.

"We've been asked to perform a survey by the leaders of our church, and that's just what we're going to do."

"Yeah, but can't we wait until this Indian war is over?" Abe asked, looking back over his shoulder.

"We don't know how long the war is going to last," I answered. "And we need the survey now."

"Who is going to want to move to a place with angry Indians everywhere?" Abe asked. "I know I wouldn't."

"This war won't last forever," I said. "I know Black Hawk. He's just got a misguided sense of what's right—at least to our way of thinking. As far as he knows, he's doing the right and noble thing by declaring war on us."

"How come you know him so well?" Abe asked, his eyes abandoning their search of the shadowed places in the brush by the roadside and settling on my face.

"When I first came to Utah, Brigham Young asked me to start a school."

"You were a schoolteacher?" Abe asked, his eyes wide. Then his brow furrowed. "I just can't picture it."

I chuckled. "Well, it's true. I was Mr. Jesse Fox, teacher of a school of white children and one Indian boy by the name of Black Hawk."

"You had Chief Black Hawk in a room full of white students and they all came out alive?"

"Of course. He's not like you think," I said, wanting Abe to understand the Black Hawk that I knew. "The kids included him in all their games until the massacre."

Abe leaned in closer. "Who did he massacre?"

"Not Black Hawk. He was just a boy. Some of the other Indians killed an entire family and stole their cattle. If the family hadn't tried to stop them they probably wouldn't have been killed."

"Yeah, what were they supposed to do, just let their livelihood walk off?"

I shook my head. I really didn't have an answer. "It was a tough situation. You've got to understand how Indians think. They figure that anything on their land that they can take is theirs. They were only trying to survive in the best way they knew how."

"So what happened?"

"About what?"

"With Black Hawk."

I opened my mouth to answer but snapped it shut when I saw the face of an Indian moving toward us.

Abe turned his head to follow my gaze. Just then, more Indians appeared from behind the trees. As soon as he saw what was coming, Abe squealed, "Lord have mercy!" and ducked his face down, wrapping his arms over his head.

"Don't show fear," I hissed.

Abe didn't answer. I could feel him trembling beside me.

"Sit up, or it will be worse for you," I said.

Abe lowered his arms and raised his head but kept his eyes down. I glanced over at him. His face was shiny with sweat and his skin had a sickly, green pallor. His chin made a prune shape as he bit down on his bottom lip so hard that I was sure he'd draw blood.

"Calm down," I said.

Abe answered in a voice so shaken that it was hard to make out the words. "So much for prayer."

Several Indians surrounded our buggy. Two of them grabbed the bridle of our horse, and the animal danced backward. Their bows were nocked with arrows; I caught sight of a spear held at the ready, its black, flint tip as dark as death. What would it feel like to have that spear buried in my heart?

The Indians probably didn't know that I could understand them as they argued back and forth. Some wanted to kill us on the spot and steal our horse and buggy. Others disagreed, and said that they should take the prize of two finely dressed white men in a horse and buggy to the chief. Some of them poked fun at Abe, calling him a woman. I was glad that he didn't know what they were saying.

Eventually, the ones who wanted to present us to their chief won the consent of the others. Our horse was taken by the reins and led away. There was no chance for us to leap to the ground and run for safety. We had mounted warriors moving along both sides of our buggy, glancing our way as they hefted their spears, clubs, and bows.

Once in camp, we were ordered to get down. Abe trembled so badly that I wasn't sure that his legs would hold him up. Several of the Indian men pointed at him and jeered. I could feel their hostility as though it were a blanket wrapped around us.

Some of the men at the edges of the group quieted and turned away. I wondered why until I saw a tall Indian approaching with dignified steps. When he got close enough, I looked into the haunting, dark eyes of Chief Black Hawk and felt myself transported back in time.

I remembered when the other kids shunned young Black Hawk after the massacre, and he chose to spend the recess break in the schoolroom with me. I opened my lunch pail and took out the starch cake that my wife, Eliza, had made for me. It was an extra-large piece. She knew how fond I was of good starch cake, and her cakes were always delicious.

I set the cake down on the desk before the lad. His eyes flew open wide in surprise, and he looked up at me.

"Look at this," I said, grinning at the boy. "The fox feeding the hawk!"

Young Black Hawk smiled for the first time since news of the massacre had reached our settlement. Sacrificing my dessert was worth seeing that smile. Besides, I could always get more cake at home. "Thank you, Mr. Fox," he said, and then he ducked his head.

In time, I rang the bell to bring the students inside. We finished our afternoon lessons, and I dismissed them. All the boys and girls scuttled out the door except for Black Hawk. He moved to the front of the room, hiding his slate behind his back and stopped in front of my desk. I looked up. He pulled the slate into view with some hesitation and turned it so I could see. There was a crude drawing of an animal with a long tail and pointed ears running along the bottom of the slate and a bird flying across the top.

"I drew this for you," Black Hawk said.

"Ah, yes, the hawk and the fox," I said, stroking my chin. "Quite an unlikely pair, wouldn't you say?"

"Both hunters," Black Hawk said. "Both friends."

"Yes," I said, standing and clapping Black Hawk on the shoulder. "Friends."

I like to think that our exchange increased Black Hawk's confidence, because he was soon playing games with the other children again.

Now I looked upon Black Hawk the man, who was taller than when I'd last seen him, with craggy features that didn't betray a shred of recognition. It had been almost twenty years since he'd been in my classroom. I had to admit that he had changed quite a bit.

Black Hawk barked an order to his men. "Put them inside."

Rough hands grabbed my arms and pushed me into a tepee. If Black Hawk had recognized me, he would have acknowledged it by now. It wasn't surprising that his anger at the white man was stronger than the memory of a single piece of cake.

Abe collapsed onto the ground inside the tepee. "They're gonna kill us," he moaned. "It's gonna be torture."

My heart quailed at the very thought of his dire prediction. I wasn't afraid of dying, but I was familiar with Indian torture methods and I didn't relish the thought of enduring any of them. A mark of manhood for Braves in warring tribes was to test how well they could tolerate their opponents tortures.

I had never aspired to die that way. Yet, whatever the Lord was willing to have happen to me, I would go through. Eventually it would be over and I would meet my maker.

Please protect us if it be thy will, I prayed. *Let them know we bear them no ill. May we, thy children, all learn to get along.* "Amen."

"You praying again?" Abe asked. "It's kind of late for that." In the dim light of the tepee, I could see him biting his lip again.

The scuffing sound of moccasins made us both turn toward the entrance to the tepee. Abe's eyes filled with abject fear as he beheld the notorious Chief Black Hawk enter our leather prison. I faced my former student and greeted him with a nod.

Black Hawk looked me for a moment, and then bent down and drew something in the dirt. I leaned closer and adjusted my spectacles to better see what he was doing. He had drawn a dog-like creature with a bushy tail and pointed ears. Without looking up at me, he moved his finger to a place above what I recognized as a fox and drew a bird with outstretched wings.

"Fox and hawk," I said.

Black Hawk rose to his feet and faced me, a smile tugging at the corners of his mouth. "Did you think I had forgotten?" he asked.

"Perhaps," I said.

"I had to get you out of the way until I could send some of my more angry and bloodthirsty warriors away," Black Hawk said. "I have told the others that you are my friend. They will escort you to the fort. You will have no further trouble."

My heart filled with gratitude. From the corner of my eye, I saw Abe looking at Black Hawk with his eyes opened wide in a mixture of hope and disbelief.

"Thank you," I said.

Black Hawk nodded and left the tepee.

I pulled Abe up off the ground and walked him out into the sunshine, but he pulled back when he caught sight of a passel of Indians surrounding our buggy, staring at us with glittering dark eyes.

"They're an escort," I reminded him.

The Indian guard parted their horses, and we climbed into the buggy and started down the mountain. The Indians moved when we moved, keeping us surrounded until we came within sight of the fort. Before we got within firing range, the Indians peeled off and disappeared into the brush.

"Thank you, dear God, for saving us," Abe whispered, his hands folded in front of him, but his wide eyes fixed on the fort ahead.

I nodded in agreement. "Amen."

Black Hawk was a student in Jesse Williams Fox's school in Manti. After an Indian massacre, the white students shunned Black Hawk, but Fox befriended him.

During the Black Hawk War of 1865–1867, Jesse Fox was riding in a wagon with Abe Doremus to survey a site. Indians surrounded the wagon until Black Hawk saw who was in it and waved them on. He appointed an Indian guard to see them to their next destination.

In another account, the captives were taken into a tepee where Black Hawk joined them later. He drew a picture of a hawk and fox in the dirt, letting his former teacher know he hadn't forgotten him, and then set the men free.

Sources: *The Manti Temple*, Manti Temple Centennial Committee (Provo, Utah: Community Press, 1988), 22; *Saga of the Sanpitch* 15 (1983): 29.

First Impressions

I had never seen a paleface, but I wanted to. My friend Lame Horse said they had strange, light eyes that were as blue as the sky or as green as deep, swirling pools of cold river water. He said that a very few of the palefaces had true eyes—eyes that were as dark as ours. I longed to see for myself the eyes of sky and water. I couldn't help but wonder how they could see. A shiver of apprehension shook my spine. One who had pale eyes could not be trusted.

Another strange feature of the whites was their hair. I knew about this firsthand because I had seen paleface scalps. Even the dark hairs were different from my people. Strands of lighter brown intermingled with dark ones, and some of their hair twisted into curves like a river. There were yellow hairs too, and once I'd seen a scalp the deep red of a fox pelt. What kind of demons were these, with colors that didn't belong on a human head? Perhaps the palefaces were more like animals than men.

When I was chosen to join a raid on the palefaces, I was both excited and nervous. I would not let anyone read those feelings on my face; if they saw what I was feeling, they would call me a mouse, and refuse to let me go.

The word had come that some of the palefaces would be moving through a narrow pass on the other side of the river. They would be strung out along the trail and more helpless in the pass than they would be on the plain, where they would circle and face out like bison guarding their young. Lame Horse said that every night the palefaces gathered in a group and counted everybody, to make sure the old and sick were keeping up. How barbaric it was that they would never leave the old or weak ones behind to either become strong or die. They kept dragging them along, prolonging their suffering and forcing them to delay their passage into the happy afterlife that awaited them. The whites were stupid.

We rode out to the pass on our swiftest horses. When we reached the hill that crested the pass, an older warrior named Tamuk told us to leave our horses so that we could scout the strangers without arousing their suspicion. I crept up the hillside behind Lame Horse, my bow over my shoulder and my arrows resting in the quiver on my back.

On the hilltop, we laid ourselves down on the ground and directed our gaze between the rocks so that the palefaces below would not see our heads. What I saw then was a sight stranger than I could have ever dreamed. The women were dressed in long skins, but the colors were unlike any animal I'd ever seen—they were the colors of sky and flowers and grass. The men wore strange little round animals crouched on their heads with wings that spread out all around them. Later, Lame Horse told me that they weren't animals at all, but hats that the whites wore to keep the sun from burning their pale skin. When Lame Horse told me that burned palefaces peeled like a snake shedding its too-small skin, I couldn't suppress a shiver.

The palefaces pushed and pulled big wooden bundles that moved along on two full moons with lines drawn through them. Although I could only see one moon shape, Lame Horse assured me that there was one on the other side as well. He called them "wheels." The white men moved their belongings on these strange carts, much like we used our travois, which were two long poles fastened to either side of a horse. The dragging ends were fastened together before loading up folded tepee skins, stone grinding bowls, extra clothing, and other items we used to survive. But we used horses to pull our travois, and if we were short of horses, our women pulled them.

Now I stared at the palefaces below us, not believing the strangest thing that they were doing. The men pulled and pushed the paleface travois right alongside the women. I'd never seen such a gathering of rabbit-hearted men in my life.

I snorted. "How can we attack men who do women's work?"

Lame Horse looked over at me, his face split in a grin of derision. "We can't fight such men. It would make us weak and without honor in our own village."

I nodded in agreement.

Tamuk shook his head, and I could hear the sounds of a chuckle rising from his throat. His amusement was contagious, and I started to laugh. Lame Horse joined me, and then the other warriors, and soon we were laughing so hard that we forgot we were supposed to be silent.

A shout from the palefaces brought us to our senses. We looked down on the travelers and saw a few of them pointing at us. Some of the women wrung their hands or covered their faces. A few ducked behind their strange travois.

A handful of men dug through the bundles in the back of their travois, but one man threw back his head and began to bray, his eyes squeezed shut with the effort. I was startled by the eerie sound, and felt a shiver run down my back.

"Hee-haw, hee-haw, hee-haw."

Others soon joined him in the most unnatural sound that I'd ever heard, which was like a pained laughter.

"They make the sound of a donkey," Lame Horse said.

"They are crazy," Tamuk said. "We must not molest them, or else their crazy spirits will follow us and torment us the rest of our lives."

I wanted nothing to do with crazy palefaces. They were frightening enough when they were sane.

I lost no time in scooting backward down the hill. As soon as I was sure that I could safely straighten up and be out of sight of their pale eyes, I stood and hurried to my horse. I swung myself up on his back and didn't even look to see if my tribesmen were following me. There was no honor in running from a fight, but there was no shame in escaping a tribe of crazy people.

Norma Pyper Mitchell, author of Prophecy Checklist, *told me these stories that were related to her by her daughter-in-law, a descendent of Shoshones, who verbally passed on the story of the time their ancestors crept up on a handcart company intent on ambush but backed off when they saw the men doing the women's work of pulling the handcarts.*

On another occasion, the Shoshones were intent on raiding a group of pioneers when one of the white men spotted the Indians and began braying like a donkey. Other pioneers joined him, and the Indians left them alone so that the crazy white men's medicine wouldn't contaminate them.

Do Unto Others

At first glance I thought it was just another log, but then I saw the toes. What I stared at was no stick, but a human leg poking out from under a bush. My heart nearly crawled out of my throat. The leg was brown, but I couldn't tell if that was its natural color or if it was dirty. The only thing I knew for sure is that the leg wasn't moving.

"Eleazer, what have you gotten yourself into this time?" I whispered. I had no way of knowing if the person attached to that foot was friendly or not. I could have kicked myself for being such a fool as to come out gathering wood alone.

I moved closer, with my rifle at the ready; my stomach turned over in somersaults just as my three-year-old, Samuel, did when he was looking for attention.

Soon I was close enough to see the dirty fringe of an Indian dress.

"Hello?"

There was no answer to my call. Now what was I supposed to do? Perhaps this woman was dead and I was on sacred burial grounds, and now I would be cursed forever. Even though part of my brain was telling me I ought to hightail it out of there, another part was compelled to see the face of this woman who'd met some unfortunate end in the wilderness.

I walked closer, angling my approach. When I could finally see her face set with high cheekbones and a slack jaw, her eyes were closed. Dead, sure enough.

Strands of her long hair were already buried in the dirt, so I couldn't be sure if the gray streaks were from old age or from the fine, gray dust that sifted through her hair.

What should I do? Should I bury her? It just didn't seem right to leave a human being lying out on the ground for the wild animals to scavenge, even if she was an Indian.

I wished I hadn't been the one to find her. Perhaps I should return to the fort and ask someone who'd been here longer what I should do. They'd been around Indians a lot more than I had.

As if I didn't have enough trouble already, the dead Indian rolled her head toward me and moaned. I was shocked into rigidity when one black eye opened and stared right at me. Then her eye closed and I was left wondering if I had actually seen the woman move. Had I looked into the blackness of her eye and seen pain and fear there?

"Hello?" I called in a voice almost too soft to be heard. It's not that I wanted to bring that single, eerie eye back to life, but I needed to know if she really was alive.

Both of her eyes opened, narrowed against the daylight, and stared a hole right through me. "Ayusta." The word was a tortured whisper, spoken through a mouth with a tongue so thick from thirst that I could barely understand her. I didn't know what it meant, of course, but maybe someone back at the fort would.

The Indian woman coughed, and I hurried back to my wagon as though the very devil himself was grabbing at my heels. I scooped up my canteen and ran back to the Indian. Her eyes were closed again, and it looked as though she had shrunken into herself—totally devoid of any hope, just waiting to die.

I knelt at her side and put the canteen to her lips. She twisted her head away, her eyes wide with alarm. But when she saw what I held and tasted the water on her tongue, she raised a hand and grabbed for the canteen. I lifted her shoulders and let her drink.

"Come with me," I said. "Let me help you."

The woman didn't seem to understand, but she didn't resist when I lifted her up onto her feet and put my arm around her to keep her from falling. I had to use both arms to support her.

We made our way to my wagon, which was mostly filled with firewood. I had no blanket with me to lay her on, so I pushed her up onto the wagon seat. She slumped over onto her side, nearly falling off in the process.

"Here, here," I said, trying to project some authority with my voice. Now that I was used to the idea that she was alive, the last thing I wanted was for her to fall to the ground and crack her skull.

It was a trick to climb onto the wagon while trying to keep her steady. I boosted myself up and stepped over her. Then I sat down and leaned her against me so that she wouldn't tumble off in the other direction.

I couldn't help but glance around before I took up the reins and started the horses toward home. What if she was being watched over by someone for some reason? I didn't see another soul, however—white or brown.

The return trip to the fort was slow. I had to keep boosting the Indian up to keep her from sliding down. She eventually slumped to the floorboards at my feet, where she jostled as we rumbled over rocks and through the wagon ruts. I couldn't stand the sight of her head bouncing up and down on the footrest. Lacking any other padding, I pulled off my shirt and wadded it up underneath her head. I couldn't tell if she was grateful or not because her eyes remained closed. Maybe the trip was killing her. What if she'd died already? I shuddered at the thought that I might now be carrying a corpse back to the fort. I slapped the reins over the backs of my team, as though, if I hurried, I might outrun the ghosts of worry that chased me.

As soon as I reached my destination, I called out, "I need help!"

Fred Scow came running. "What did you drag in?" he asked, staring down at the Indian crumpled at my feet.

"I found her just lying out there," I said, flinging my arm back in the direction I'd come from.

"You should have left her," Frank said, backing up a step.

"How could I?" I asked. "She was alive when I found her, and thirsty."

"Well, she don't look thirsty now," Frank said. "She looks beyond thirsty. I think she's dead."

I climbed down from the wagon just as my wife, Mary Caroline, came hurrying over, her skirt lifted in her hands just enough for her to run without tripping. "Eleazer, what is going on?" she asked. Her eyes found the Indian woman lying in the wagon. "Who is that?"

I shrugged.

"How did she get in your wagon?"

"I put her there."

"Oh, for heaven's sake, don't just stand there, bring the poor woman into the house."

"What if she's dead?" I asked.

Mary Caroline did a quick survey of the body with her eyes and touched the woman's throat. "She's not dead—not yet anyway. Bring her in, Eleazer. There's no time to waste."

I turned to the Indian and tugged at her. "Somebody help me," I said. A couple of men who had gathered to see what was going on helped me pull the Indian off the wagon and carry her into my house.

"Nothing good can come of this," Frank said.

"Why not?" I asked, tired of his pessimism.

"Last year, Sarah Ellen Cox saved Chief Walkara's mother after he stabbed her seven times."

I recoiled in horror. "What?"

Frank shrugged. "It's the Indian way. When someone is either old or too sick to contribute to the tribe any longer, they are put out to die. They figure it's the natural order of things. They don't usually hurry them on their way like Chief Walkara—that's just something he came up with on his own. They usually just lay them out on the ground, like this one you found here, and let the elements take care of them."

"Put her on the bed," Mary Caroline instructed. We laid the Indian on my bed. "Now, out."

"Out?"

"Yes, go, shoo, shoo!" Mary Caroline flapped her hands at us, and I turned to go. Before I stepped outside, though, I swept our small cabin with my eyes. "Where's Samuel?"

"He's playing at the Miller's," Mary Caroline answered. "You can keep busy by unloading the wood." She shut the door behind me.

I went to do my wife's bidding.

By the time Mary Caroline let me back in, the Indian looked like a different person, laid out in one of Mary's old night-gowns—faded and soft from wear. Mary Caroline had even washed the Indian and braided her hair. The Indian's face looked even browner next to the white pillow slip.

"Now, tell me how you found her," Mary Caroline said.

After I told her everything, Mary Caroline said, "She must have gotten sick and been left to die."

I shuddered inside. I couldn't imagine leaving Mary Caroline lying on the ground no matter how sick she was.

"What's ailing her?" I asked.

"I'm not sure, but she feels hot. Whether that's from lying in the sun or from fever, I just don't know."

In the afternoon of the next day, the Indian woke up. She soon tired of the broth that Mary Caroline tried to spoon-feed her and graduated to bread. She ate everything we gave her and some things that she helped herself to. She drank a lot of water, and guzzled milk. When I complained, Mary Caroline said, " It's good for her."

"It's good for Samuel too."

"It's all right, Eleazer," Mary Caroline said. "There's enough."

The Indian watched our exchange. Then she said the same word she'd said up in the foothills: "Ayusta."

"I think that's her name," I said.

"It's kind of pretty," Mary Caroline agreed. So we called her Ayusta.

Later on, Fred told me that "ayusta" meant "abandoned." The name seemed to fit.

At first, Samuel was afraid of the dark-skinned woman lying in our bed. Ayusta watched Samuel from her nest of pillows, her black eyes brimming with merriment. When he decided to ignore her and go about his usual play, she pointed at him. "Ha!" she said, laughing at his antics.

Samuel soon learned that there was nothing to fear from Ayusta, and he grew fond of her. He climbed onto the bed and let her pat his blonde hair. Somehow, Ayusta communicated to Mary Caroline that she wanted some straw, which she used to braid a little straw horse for Samuel. He watched her closely, but not until it was nearly finished did he recognize what it was.

"Horsey!" he exclaimed in delight. When Ayusta gave him the toy, Samuel gave her a hug in return.

"Samuel, what do you say?" Mary Caroline prompted.

"T'ank you!" Samuel said.

"T'ank you!" Ayusta repeated, grinning from ear to ear.

The straw horse became Samuel's favorite plaything. He was so fond of it that he even slept with it.

After a couple of weeks, Ayusta was up and about—poking into this and that, tasting everything, and following Mary Caroline everywhere she went. She picked up some English words, and taught Samuel a few words of the Indian language.

A little while later, some Indians came to the fort, looking to trade skins for cloth and flour. When Ayusta saw the women who carried the bundles they had to trade, she squealed and spoke to them in her native tongue.

"These are her friends," Fred told me. "She wants to go back with them."

"What if she gets sick again?" I asked.

"They'll probably abandon her again. It's just their way." He shot me a look. I must have had a pained expression on my face, because he said, "They probably don't understand the things we do either."

Ayusta left with her friends, talking and laughing as they made their way back across the foothills to their camp. I wondered if she was talking about her rescue, Samuel's antics, or the kindness of my wife.

With Ayusta gone, I thought our adventure was over, but I was wrong. The worst was yet to come.

Samuel was an inquisitive boy who was hard-pressed to sit still for even a minute. He'd hardly ever listen to a story all the way through, preferring to act out his own adventures, and he would squirm and wiggle at bedtime every night until the very moment he dropped off to sleep.

Samuel loved to go with me whenever I ventured outside the fort, but I only took him when I knew I could keep an eye on him. There were too many things that could go wrong in this untamed wilderness. We had to deal with wild animals, Indians, creeks, cliffs, and rattlesnakes, which were all potentially dangerous to a little boy.

One day when I was going out hunting, Samuel begged to go with me. I knew I couldn't keep a proper watch on him and hope to bag any game, so I told him that I'd take him to gather wood when I got back. I meant that we would go to gather wood the next day, but Samuel must have been thinking of going the moment I returned. I didn't know his intentions at the time, or I would have told him to go back into the house with his mother instead of allowing him to stand by the gate and watch me ride away from the fort.

I turned around three or four times to wave to Samuel, seeing my boy grow smaller and smaller, but he always lifted his little hand to wave back. Finally, I kicked my horse into a gallop and was soon out of sight.

I was lucky that day—I got a deer. I was feeling mighty happy when I rode back to the fort at dusk. I imagined Mary Caroline sitting at home waiting for me, her hair loose and full around her face, and little Samuel tucked into bed, his cheeks rosy from play. I was mighty content until I rode into the fort and saw Mary Caroline waiting for me, her face streaked with tears. I slid off my horse, the deer forgotten in my concern.

"What's the matter?" I asked.

"Samuel . . ." she said and then broke down crying.

I took my wife by the shoulders and stared into her face. "Where's Samuel?"

"He's gone. An Indian took him." Mary covered her face

with her hands and wept.

The image of my little boy waving from beside the open gate of the fort twisted my stomach into a hard knot. Why had I thought he'd be safe? Why did I think he'd take himself home once I was out of sight? Why didn't I insist that he go home while I watched? He was just a baby. What had I been thinking?

My chest hurt. How terrified Samuel must be! What must it be like for him—stolen from his family and suffering who-knew-what at the hands of the Indians?

I hugged Mary Caroline, but it wasn't enough comfort to keep the sting of tears from my eyes. "I'll find him," I whispered through gritted teeth. No one was going to keep my son from me. I would find Samuel or die in the attempt.

I felt a hand on my shoulder. "We're with you, Eleazer," said Fred Scow.

"We're assembling a posse that will leave first thing in the morning."

"I don't want to wait."

"We have to. We can't find him in the dark."

I didn't sleep that night—I couldn't. I cleaned my gun, packed my ammunition, and thought of Samuel.

At first light I was mounted and ready. A dozen men were with me, leaving their fields unworked and their animals untended just to help me search for my son, but there was no room in my heart for gratitude yet. We had to find Samuel first—that's all I cared about.

The gate swung open and I kicked my horse into a trot. Almost immediately, I slowed, and then stopped when I saw Ayusta stumbling toward me, clutching a blanket in her arms. Her face was ruddy from exertion, and her mouth hung open as she breathed in large gulps of air.

"'Leazer," she called. "Here Samuel." She stopped and squatted down, peeling back the blanket to reveal the face of my son. His eyes were closed and his face was pale. For one heart-stopping moment, I thought he was dead. Then Samuel yawned and stretched.

I leapt off my horse and dashed over to scoop him up into my arms.

"Samuel! Samuel! Oh, my son," I cried.

"Papa!" Samuel said, and wrapped both of his little arms around my neck.

I stared at Ayusta, unashamed of the tears that ran down my face. "Thank you, thank you." I whispered.

"How'd she do that?" Fred asked.

"I don't know," I said.

Ayusta started speaking rapidly in her tongue. I didn't care what she had to say. All I cared about was that I had Samuel back.

At last Fred nodded and smiled. Then he turned to me.

"Samuel must have gone out chasing rabbits while he waited for you to come back to take him wood gathering. Seems that the brave who took Samuel is part of her tribe. The Indian rode into camp with him yesterday, and Samuel cried himself to sleep last night. When Ayusta was sure that everyone in camp was asleep, she snuck into the tepee where Samuel slept and rescued him. She's walked most of the night to bring him back to you."

My eyes filled with tears even as my heart swelled with gratitude. "Thank you, Ayusta. Come with me." I motioned with my hand for her to follow. "We'll see Mary Caroline, get some food, and let you rest."

Ayusta grinned. "T'ank you," she said, following me into the fort.

In 1855, Eleazer King found an Indian woman in the foothills where she'd been left to die. He took her back to the fort, where his wife, Mary Caroline, was instrumental in nursing her back to health. The squaw became especially fond of three-year-old Samuel King.

When the Indian was well again, she returned to her tribe. One day not long after, Samuel chased rabbits outside the fort until he was far enough away that an Indian brave swooped down on his horse and stole the child, carrying the screaming toddler back to his camp.

In the dark of night, the Indian woman who'd been cared for by Mary Caroline King stole Samuel from the tepee where he'd cried himself to sleep and carried him back to the fort to return him to his grateful parents.

Sources: Guy Wetzel, *Samuel Eleazor King History,* oral account of his ancestor Sarah Ellen Jones Cox, who saved Chief Walker's mother after the chief had stabbed her seven times; *Saga of the Sanpitch* 12 (1980): 1.

Topaddie's Treasure

I was the first one to see the Indian stalking down the road. My heart leaped up in my chest, even though I knew that the Indians weren't always looking for a fight. He had no bow and arrow that I could see, nor was his face painted with war paint.

When the Indian drew closer, I recognized him as someone my father knew, even though I couldn't remember his name. They all looked pretty much alike to me. They sounded alike too—all gibberish. Pa could communicate with them, though, a fact that made me proud.

When the Indian reached me, he stooped down and rested on his haunches like a grasshopper settling down in the weeds. "Where Cox?" he asked in his guttural English.

"Uh, do you mean Will?" I stuttered. I had several older brothers and my father who were all Cox. I was Cox, for that matter, but I didn't think that this Indian would have any business with a nine-year-old boy—I gulped—at least I hoped he didn't. Indians were known to kidnap children and take them either to their tepees to raise as their own or else to sell in the slave trade. Surely he would know better than to try to take a child of Orville Cox. Dad was always fair with the Indians and generous to boot. He was nicer to them than a lot of folks thought he ought to be, but Papa didn't care what other people thought.

"Me see Father Cox," the Indian said.

I jumped up and went running into the house to get my Pa. He heard my feet before he saw me. "Walter, running is for outside, not in."

"But there's an Indian to see you, Pa."

Pa's gaze went past me, although he couldn't see the Indian

from there. "All right, let's go see what he wants."

I followed Pa out to the yard and heard him say, "Hello, Topaddie." Topaddie sniffed the air loudly, and then placed a hand over his stomach.

"Come and eat with us," Pa said.

Topaddie started for the house, but Pa called him back and led the way toward the stream. "First, we wash," Pa said.

I knelt by the stream next to Pa and watched him work a hard bar of yellow soap around and around his hands in the water. Then he handed the bar to Topaddie. The Indian looked from the soap to Pa and back again. He sniffed the soap. It was obvious that he didn't know what to do with it.

"Here," I said, holding out my hand. "I wash, too." Topaddie surrendered the soap. I showed him how I washed my hands, and then gave it back to him.

Topaddie dipped the soap down into the water and worked it around inside his hands in an awkward imitation of what Pa and I had done.

"That's fine," Pa said, smiling his approval.

We went inside and sat around the table with the family. Pa set an example by folding his arms and bowing his head. Topaddie looked around at all of our bowed heads before he lowered his own.

Pa began one of his prayers where he thanked Heavenly Father for everything and asked a blessing on everyone. I knew I was supposed to keep my eyes closed, but I couldn't help peeking at Topaddie. I saw him glance up at the food on the table more than once and then turn a questioning eye on Pa before he bowed his head again. I nearly laughed out loud when Topaddie's stomach growled loud enough to nearly drown out Pa's words.

At last Pa finished his prayer, and we passed the bowls around. Soon there was not a crumb left, except for the heel of bread that Topaddie held in his hand. He grabbed the soup pot from the middle of the table and swiped the bread around the inside. We all gasped at his bad manners and threw a glance at Ma. She turned her head away.

Topaddie stuffed the bread in his mouth all at once, and then chewed and swallowed. He let a belch rumble out of his throat, and then grinned at Ma. My sisters gasped, and Ma stood up and moved over to stand at the stove.

"Plenty good," Topaddie said.

"Come on, Topaddie, let's talk." Pa pushed away from the table, and Topaddie stood up with the awkward movement of one who is not used to sitting on a chair. The chair toppled over behind him, and Topaddie jumped away from it, startled.

"I'll get it." I got up and lifted the fallen chair back to its place. Then, when the rest of the children were clearing the table, I snuck out the door and went in search of Pa and the Indian.

Pa sat on a porch chair, and Topaddie seated himself on the floor beside him. Pa didn't seem to find this strange at all.

"I find wagons, left from white man in hats with long sticks that spit fire," Topaddie said.

Pa sat up straighter. "Johnston's Army?"

"Yes, army. You come with me, I show you."

"They still have their wheels?"

Topaddie nodded, a pleased grin on his face. "Yes."

"Where are they?"

"Green River."

"How many?"

Topaddie held up two fingers.

"Hmm. That's a pretty far piece, near 200 miles. I need to think this over. Come tomorrow and I'll give you my answer."

Topaddie shot a look at the kitchen door and grinned. "I come tomorrow, same time," he said. The Indian rose to his feet and rubbed his distended belly.

"Good-bye," Pa said before he went back inside in search of Ma. I followed him.

"Topaddie told me of some wagons that the army left behind out by Green River," Pa said.

"You're not going after them alone, are you?" Ma asked.

"I'll go with him," I said, my heart beating hard with anticipation.

Ma looked at me, her eyes round with disbelief. "It might be dangerous," she said.

"I think that if I can find someone else to go along and help me out that Walter might as well come along too," Pa said.

Ma stared at him, her mouth open as though she was trying to catch a fly.

"After all, Walt is nearly a man," Pa said, ignoring Ma's expression.

Pa ended up talking Archie Buchanan into going with him to fetch the wagons. "There ought to be lots of valuable iron left on those wagons," Brother Buchanan said.

"I wouldn't go if I didn't think it was worth it," Pa said.

It was hard to wait for Topaddie to come back the next evening. I was ready to go right now. I was so excited that I almost couldn't stand it.

Topaddie finally came into sight along the road, his smile visible from several yards away.

"Cox here?" he asked. I ran to get Pa.

"Topaddie, welcome," Pa said. "Come and eat with us." This time, Topaddie headed for the stream without any prompting from Pa. Either he was a fast learner of the white man's ways or he was mighty hungry.

Supper went much like the night before, with Topaddie soaking up the leftovers again. I wondered if he ate this much back at his own camp.

Since we'd already decided to go, it was mighty disappointing to me to find out that it would take a few days to get provisioned for the trip. We had to pack food, water, and round up a couple of teams of horses to pull the wagons back to town. More than once, I heard Ma question Pa about taking me. She said he ought to take one of the older boys instead.

"No, Elvira, I'm going to take Walter. Will and the other boys need to keep the place running while I'm gone. Will's just the right age for an adventure."

At last we set out on our journey, riding the horses that would pull the wagons back home. We had a team from our farm, and one that belonged to Archie Buchanan. There was a horse for each of us, and Topaddie sat proudly on his. Mine had the most provisions. Since there would be stretches without any readily available water, we had to pack some of that too. I wondered if my horse even knew I was up here on his back because I surely didn't weigh as much as the gear he was carrying.

After a day or two of traveling, I couldn't sit still but not because I was excited. It was because my backside was sore! I'd ridden horses around the farm plenty of times before but never for this long in one stretch.

I was grateful for the evenings when we stopped to camp and I could get off my horse and walk around for a bit.

After riding for so long that I wondered if we'd ever get there, Topaddie stopped and looked around, a frown of puzzlement plain on his face.

Pa sat forward on his horse and asked, "What's wrong?"

"The wagons," Topaddie said. "They're gone."

Pa's eyebrows shot up and he scanned the ground. "Are you sure?" he asked. "They were right here?"

"Sure," Topaddie said, his answer sounding more like a question.

We searched for those wagons for two days. Finally, we spotted them in the distance, under a tree.

Topaddie whooped. "Here they are! Under tree, by big rock, just where I left them!"

The wagons were big, heavy things, typical of the United States Army. I'd never seen any before, but I'd heard stories. The army had left Utah and gone back to some war they were having in the east. Dragging these wagons, empty of provisions, must have seemed like too much effort for horses and oxen that still had a fair piece to go.

Pa examined the wheels and axles. One wheel had broken spokes, and it took three days to get the wagons road-worthy. Finally, we headed back toward home.

Pa said that the unexpected delay had depleted our food supply. I thought it was more Topaddie's fault, since he ate so much. Even though we had half of what we started out with, Pa explained that pulling the heavy wagons home would take longer than our ride out to find them. As soon as I heard that Pa was planning on rationing our food to one meal a day, I checked underneath the canvas wagon covers, hoping to find some left-behind Army food or provisions. There weren't any. The canvas covers flapped their tattered edges at me in derision.

My stomach rebelled against having only one meal a day, biting at my belly with sharp pains of protest, but there wasn't anything I could do about it. I rode on the wagon seat beside Pa, my bones jolting with each thump of the metal-rimmed wheels over rocks and ruts.

Topaddie often ranged far a field on foot. It's a good thing he was used to getting around that way because with the horses pulling the wagons, they were no longer available for side trips.

One evening when we got close to a camping place, we noticed Topaddie crouched down in the distance. When we drew near, I caught the welcome scent of fresh roasting meat.

As soon as Pa pulled to a halt, I scrambled down from the wagon seat. Topaddie grinned up at me. Lying before him in a small bed of hot coals was the carcass of a rabbit. Even though it didn't look like much, I grinned back at him. Some was better than none.

After the horses were taken care of, Topaddie divided the rabbit between us. I noticed that he gave us the meat and kept the entrails for himself. I didn't watch him eat but rather turned away and chewed and swallowed my portion with a grateful heart.

There were some steep spots in the trail that we'd ridden over on our journey out without a second thought, but on the way back, we had to double the horses so they could pull a single wagon up the incline. We'd have to put rocks behind the wagon's wheels once it reached the top, and then walk the horses back down the hill and hook them up to the next wagon. In a way, it was a good thing that the wagons were empty, or else our four tired horses wouldn't have been enough to get them up and over the steep inclines.

I was glad that Topaddie continued to find game from time to time, trotting out to where I couldn't even see him and catching up to us later in the day. I especially liked it when he got some animal for us to eat, but even the roots and berries he brought us were welcome. I was sorely missing Mama's flour biscuits, but I would never say that to Topaddie. He was keeping me alive, and I was grateful.

When we finally rolled into town, I was never more glad to see my family. I hopped off the wagon, intent on heading for the house and some of Mama's real food, when Pa stopped me. "We've got to see to the animals, son."

At first, I thought Pa was being awfully hard on me, but then I realized that Pa would expect the same of my big brothers. So I squared my shoulders, took one of the horses, and led it into the barn.

When the animals were settled, we washed our hands and went in to dinner. Topaddie was there, of course, having been the instrument of our family's good fortune. He was the most talkative, speaking around mouthfuls of food while Pa and I just kept shoveling it in.

When Mama asked how the trip was, Topaddie was the one who answered. "Good," he said. "But Cox no wash much."

An Indian named Topaddie came to the Orville Cox house in 1862 with news that he'd found two wagons abandoned by Johnston's Army on its way to the Civil War. They were near Green River, a distance of about 180 miles. Cox invited his friend Archie Buchanan to help him bring in the bounty. Although Orville Cox had a son named Walter, he didn't really go on the wagon rescue mission. I added him so that he could take us along on the adventure.

Sources: Milton R. Hunter, *Utah Indian Stories* (Springville, Utah: Art City Publishing, 1946).

Sick, Sick, Sick

"Lena, the wheel came off my buggy again," Florence whined.

Despite my promise to Mama, I was growing impatient. "Well, then, just carry your doll," I said.

Honestly, sometimes I wondered how Florence could be my real sister. She was so dumb. I was embarrassed to be related to her.

"But I want my buggy!" she cried, the word "buggy" rising up into a teeth-rattling wail.

"Oh, for Pete's sake. I'll fix your buggy," Dorothy snapped.

My eyebrows went up in surprise at her harsh tone of voice. Usually Dorothy was the quiet one—the peacemaker who got in between Florence and me and begged us to get along.

I wiped my face with the back of my hand. It came away wet with sweat and dirty with dust from the road. I didn't figure that Mama would approve if she had been here to see me. But she and Pa had gone to the mill, and I had promised her that I would take good care of Florence and Dorothy. That meant playing, as far as I was concerned. I knew that there were plenty of chores to do, but I reasoned that they would still be there when Mama got back and insisted that we get to work.

Right now, we were playing mommies out in the yard, and we each had our own doll to mother. Mine was the prettiest, of course. Dorothy's was next prettiest, and Florence's was downright ugly. When I really wanted to get her goat, I would tell her how ugly it was. I would never resort to such tactics unless I was mad enough that I didn't care about hearing her whine.

Dorothy picked up the buggy wheel. Florence watched her

with a scowl on her face. When Dorothy pulled the buggy up on one side to inspect the axel, Florence shrieked, "You'll dump Maybelle out!"

I was irritated, I'll own up to it. That was the reason I said, "Well, if she hits the ground with her face, it might improve her looks."

Florence really opened up at that, the tears pouring down her face as her mouth opened wide enough to fit both of her fists inside. She screamed and cried as though an ox had just stepped on her foot. I would have liked to step on her tongue. Instead, I plugged my ears and then pulled my fingers out partway before pushing them in again. I pulled them out and pushed them in as rapidly as I could. It gave Florence's cry a wobble that was rather amusing. It was even better when I closed my eyes so that I didn't have to look at her.

I thought I heard Dorothy say something like, "Hush, now!" but it was indistinct in the warble of Florence's screams.

After a moment, someone pushed on my shoulder. I dropped my hands from my ears and my eyes flew open to see Dorothy standing in front of me, her face the picture of horror.

I'm the first to admit that Florence's crying is bad, but I thought Dorothy was exaggerating a bit. Her expression was positively unnerving.

"Stop it!" I snapped.

"Look!" Dorothy said, pointing to something over my shoulder. When I turned around to see, I started screaming myself. A half dozen Indians walked toward us from the foothills. By their bare chests I knew they were men, and from the weapons they carried I knew that I'd better be scared.

Indians stole kids like us. They killed kids too. One time an Indian had tried to sell a little Indian slave child to Brother Morley, and Brother Morley said he didn't want to buy a child. So the Indian picked the child up by the feet, swung him up over his head, and dashed the kid's head on the ground, killing him just like that.

I didn't want to be any Indian's sledgehammer, so I turned

and ran for the house, grabbing Florence's hand along the way. After all, I had promised Mama I'd take good care of her. Dorothy's footsteps sounded right behind me, her heavy breathing hot on my neck. We stumbled inside the house and slammed the door shut.

"Hush your mouth!" I snapped at Florence. "Stop screaming or they'll find us! Do you want to have your brains dashed out? Not that it would make that much of a mess."

Florence clutched my hand tighter and quieted some, but she still caught little sobs between breaths.

The sound irritated me. I knew we weren't safe yet. If you didn't answer your door when the Indians knocked, they just went ahead and let themselves in. Sometimes they didn't bother knocking at all. They had no respect for property or privacy. They figured that a thing belonged to whoever had it, or whoever could steal it—and kids were things.

"Shut up, Florence, you're making me sick!" I hissed.

Actually, it was knowing that the Indians were getting closer and closer with each passing moment that was twisting my guts up in fear.

Dorothy tapped my shoulder.

"Stop that!" I screamed.

"I have an idea," Dorothy said. "Let's get in bed and pull the covers up."

"That is so stupid," I said. "You think they won't look under the covers for us?"

"No," Dorothy said. "That's not what I mean. We should pretend to be sick. I heard Pa say that the Indians think our sickness is bad medicine. Evelyn Carlson's mother told her to put red spots on her face if she ever saw an Indian coming to their house. They won't get close to sick white people. If we're sick, they'll be scared of us and leave us alone."

I looked down at my two little sisters. Imagining that the Indians could possibly be scared of them was difficult, but what else could we do?

"Okay," I said. "Let's be sick."

I made a dash for the big bed just off the front room that Mama and Papa slept in. I didn't even bother to take off my shoes. I just jumped into that bed and pulled the covers up to my chin.

Dorothy followed, dragging Florence with her. Florence was crying again.

I scooted to the middle so that my sisters would have to get in on either side. If Dorothy's plan didn't work and one of us got snatched, I wanted to make darn sure it wasn't me.

"Quit crying, Florence. Start coughing," I said.

Florence muffled her face in Pa's pillow and tried a cough or two. They weren't very convincing.

Dorothy did a better job of it. Her coughs shook the bed.

I gave it a try and found that coughing too hard hurt my throat. So, I did my part by letting out a dry, whispery cough that sounded like it belonged to someone's old grandma.

It seemed like forever before a knock sounded on the door. My heart rattled in fear, and I coughed all the harder. I'd rather have a sore throat than end up missing my brains through a hole in my head.

I shivered for real when I heard the door squeak open. I wanted to look but didn't dare.

Florence wasn't doing her share of the coughing, so I nudged her with my elbow. She squealed in fear and buried her face in Pa's pillow again. Her cry could have been mistaken for a cough—if you had a real good imagination.

Deep, guttural voices raised in argument before the door shut with a blessed *bang!*

Still, I didn't dare look. What if the Indians had come inside and shut the door behind them? What if they knew we were faking? Maybe they were standing on either side of the bed right now, knives drawn, ready to collect our scalps because we weren't any good to them alive if we were sick.

Dorothy grabbed my shoulder and I nearly died of fright. "They're gone," she said. "We can get up now."

I collapsed into the mattress tick and stopped coughing. My throat thanked me.

"I don't want to get up," I said. "I feel sick."

McKay Andreason told me the story of how his grandmother Anne Lena Frandsen Andreason pretended to be sick in bed with her two sisters when they were home alone and saw Indians coming down out of the mountains.

Merilyn Jorgensen told me the story of her mother, Evelyn Carlson Anderson, who was instructed to always check to see who was knocking. If it was an Indian, she had to dot her face with red lip rouge before she opened the door because the Indians were so afraid of white men's diseases that they wouldn't bother her if she was sick.

Bought and Paid for

The Indian boy stood with his head down, his greasy hair hanging around his shoulders in hopeless, black tangles. His face was so dark that I couldn't tell if it was his natural skin color or if it was from the dirt that streaked his body.

His captor prodded him forward, and the boy stumbled. It was then that I noticed his ribs showing plainly through his dusky skin. A rope circled the boy's chest, pinning his upper arms to his sides. I wondered when he'd last had anything to eat.

"You buy," the Indian said to Pa, lifting the other end of the rope while his horse waited, one hoof tipped forward to rest.

I glanced up at the warrior and wondered if he'd made the boy walk at the end of the rope for miles and miles while he rode the horse and pulled him along. I wondered what it would be like to be stolen and forced to go to a strange place, never to see my family again. I took a step closer to Pa. Even though I was twelve years old and could do a man's work out in the fields, I knew I was no match for a full grown Indian.

"Where is he from?" Pa asked.

The Indian stuck his arm out toward the south. "Paiute," he said.

I knew enough about the Paiutes to know that they were gatherers—a peaceful people who did their best to live off the land. They didn't even have horses, so they couldn't put up much of a fight when the stronger tribes came riding down on them to take their children or anything else away from them. Thinking about it made me scared and mad at the same time.

This was the first time Pa had been approached about buying an Indian child. It was pretty common to have Indians sell children from other tribes to the whites. At first, the settlers were horrified at the idea and refused to buy them, but when the slave children were killed right before their eyes, the whites relented and the Indians knew they had a lucrative market with the palefaces.

The boy for sale looked about my age. I wondered if he ate raw meat. He sure didn't wear much. If he was going to live at our house, he'd have to get dressed or Ma wouldn't let him in. Maybe Pa would just buy him and let him go. Then he could go back to his family, and maybe he'd know better than to get caught next time.

I looked up at Pa and saw his eyes fixed on the boy. There was a softness there that I recognized from times when he was feeling proud or sorry for one of us kids. He had looked like that after my baby brother John died just one month past. I knew that Mama's heart was aching for her little boy, and I missed him too, but I sure hoped that Pa wasn't thinking that he could fill the hole John's death left in our hearts by bringing this scruffy Indian into our family.

It seemed to me that Pa was fixing to buy this boy.

"So, Pa," I said. "Don't you think the Larsen's would like to buy themselves an Indian?"

Pa didn't even look at me. "No," he said. "I think that I would like to."

Maybe Pa was thinking that he had to re-stock the Brown family's store of boys in general, since there were only two of us left, and Neuman was a grown man of twenty who had moved out of the house.

I barely remembered my other brothers who had met untimely deaths. Fred died when I was only six years old. He'd been almost three times as old as me, so my memories of him weren't clear. Then there was William, who had been dead for going on four years. He was eighteen when he died, and as much a man in my eyes as Papa was. I remembered Mama crying her eyes out, but she got over it.

I was sorry that this skinny boy had been kidnapped and all, but it wasn't my doing. I didn't know why we had to put up with him just because he was in the wrong place at the wrong time.

"Pa?"

"Robert." Pa's voice carried a warning that there was to be no more argument from me. Even though I wanted to tell him not to buy this boy on my account, because I didn't mind being the only boy left at home, I closed my mouth and watched Pa pull out his money pouch. It was heavy from the pay he'd just gotten for serving in the Mormon Battalion. He opened the bag and pulled out a gold coin. It was stamped with a shield on one side and a cross on the other. I couldn't read the words on it, on account of them being written in Spanish. I groaned inwardly at the thought of all the licorice whips that gold would buy—enough to last my lifetime. And Pa was going to waste it on an Indian.

Pa handed the Indian captor the gold piece. The Indian took it but didn't even bother to look at it. "More," he said, holding out his other hand.

Indians didn't have any use for money itself. You couldn't eat it, you couldn't wear it, and you couldn't trap an animal with it. But they had soon learned that white men would trade valuable things for the yellow metal—things that the Indians could use. They thought whites were crazy to value the small, hard pieces of gold and silver, but they were willing to take them to trade for things they wanted.

To my horror, Pa pulled out two more pieces of gold and handed them over.

"More," the Indian said.

I wanted to grab the money bag and run, to save what was left, but I knew I'd be in trouble if I did. It was Pa's money. He moved his hand to the money bag again. To my relief, he pulled the drawstring and closed it up tight. "No," Pa said. "Twenty-five dollars is enough."

The Indian looked from Pa to his captive and back again, trying to gauge if he could push for any more. Pa stared him straight in the eye.

The Indian must have figured that some was better than none

because he handed Pa the loose end of the rope and mounted his horse. He rode away without a single backward look.

The first thing Pa did was untie the rope and lift it off the boy. My stomach turned over in revulsion when I saw the places where the rope had rubbed the skin off, making bloody stripes around the boy's arms. I shivered, wondering if the boy would run now that he was free, but he didn't. He stood with his head down and his shoulders slumped.

"Come with me," Pa said, his voice as gentle as when he'd spoken to my sick little brother before he died.

The Indian boy shuffled forward on his bare feet and followed us home.

Mama turned into a regular mother hen when she saw the boy. "James, the poor child is filthy," she said. "Help me get him washed."

"First things first," Pa said. "He needs feeding worse than he needs cleaning."

Mama hurried around the kitchen getting food ready, speaking kindly to the Indian boy the whole time. After he was fed, Mama got Pa to help her fill the washtub. Pa managed to get the boy into the bath, but it was plain to see that he didn't like it any. He sat and shivered and held his arms in close to his body. Mama had Pa wash his hair, and she stood ready with a pair of scissors. When she started snipping, the Indian boy gripped his head in his hands and cried out.

"It won't hurt," Pa assured him.

At last, Mama got enough black hair cut off to satisfy herself. She told me to run get some of my clothes for the boy. I went, grumbling the whole way. When I got back, I saw Mama wrapping clean white bandages around the boy's bloody arms.

That night when we gathered for scripture reading and prayers, the Indian sat apart from us, his eyes on the floor. He was a strange sight wearing my shirt and trousers with his short hair. My sisters couldn't stop looking back and forth between us. I wanted to shout at them and say, "Stop looking at me!" but I didn't.

Pa opened the scriptures and then he paused. "We want to welcome the newest member of our family," he said. "We need to call him something. Any ideas for a name?"

"How about John?" my sister Mary Ann said.

"No!" I said, my back stiffening in protest. "Not John." John was my brother's name, and this Indian was no brother of mine.

Pa turned to me. "What do you suggest?"

I looked around the room and my eyes fell on the scriptures. We'd been reading about Alma in the court of wicked King Noah from the Book of Mormon. Maybe because this Indian boy had so recently been hunted, just like King Noah's men were doing to Alma, I said, "Alma. Call him Alma."

"That's a fine name, son," Pa said.

Mama turned to the Indian and said, "Your name is Alma."

The boy shook his head. He said one word, "Shock," the first thing I'd ever heard him say.

My older sister Sarah said, "Shock? That must be his name."

Mama frowned. "I'm not going to call him Shock." The Indian looked up at her with recognition in his eyes.

"Alma Shock Brown," Pa said, his voice firm with authority.

Alma Shock was sent to school with me, although I didn't see what good it did. He just sat there and didn't say anything.

Over time, however, Alma Shock warmed up to us. He even quit flinching any time Mama or Pa reached for him. He learned to speak our language, and he taught me Indian words. I was pretty proud of being able to speak Indian, although I didn't learn Alma's language as well as he learned English.

Alma liked living with us—I knew because he told me so. He didn't ever want to go back to digging for worms to eat and going hungry most of the winter. He liked licorice whips as much as I did, maybe even more. He didn't care for peppermints, though; he was more partial to horehound candy.

As the years passed, it seemed as though Alma had always been part of our family. He grew to manhood, and in 1861 he married Betsy Peacock, the adopted Indian daughter of Judge George Peacock.

Alma was handy to have around when it came to Indian communication. He would often act as a go-between, trying for peace that was long in coming. Most Indian children were sold to the whites at a very young age and didn't have much memory of their birthplace, but Alma was half grown when he was captured, so he remembered his language and his life among the Indians. When the Black Hawk War broke out a couple of years later, Alma used his unique position of being an Indian raised by whites to work between the warring factions.

There was that memorable day when Alma Shock learned that Christian Anderson had been captured from where he'd been working in his field. The other men with him had been killed outright.

Alma didn't hesitate to ride his pony up the mountain, hot on the trail of the marauding Indians. He found Christian Anderson tied to a post. The Indians were preparing to torture and kill him, to make him suffer for all of the Indians who had been slain during the war.

Alma Shock managed to convince the Indians that Christian was a good man, and not one of those who had raided and killed Indian women and children. The Indians set their captive free.

It turned out that twenty-five dollars was a real bargain for my brother Alma Shock Brown.

Ruth Davenport Scow's great-grandparents James "Polly" and Eunice Reasor Brown paid $25 for an Indian youth in the 1850s. They treated the boy, named Alma Shock Brown, like a son. He grew and married another adopted Indian named Betsy Peacock. Alma Shock Brown acted as a go-between for whites *and Indians during the Black Hawk War. He rescued Christian Anderson from certain death when he convinced Christian's captors that he was a good man, and the Indians let him go.*

Source: *Saga of the Sanpitch* 27 (1995): 23.

A Fair Trade

I was brushing my best horse, a fine three-year-old stallion, when I heard footsteps behind me.

I turned to see an Indian brave move up to the rail fence that surrounded the paddock where I stood. I kept a hold on the stallion's lead rope and gave my visitor a friendly nod. "Hello," I said.

I wasn't alarmed. I didn't feel I had any need to be. Indians were a common sight, and we generally got along.

An Indian woman, who I assumed was the brave's wife, trailed behind him with a young child cradled in her arms. She halted when she was a respectful distance behind the Indian brave. She boosted her child up on her hip and pointed to my horse with a slender brown finger. She whispered something into her baby's ear.

The child grinned, its dark eyes squinting in sheer delight. The mother smiled at her baby with such tenderness that it lifted my heart and spread a smile across my face.

The Indian grunted. "Fine horse," he said.

"Yes," I agreed, turning back to admire my stallion's glossy brown coat. He was a beauty—full of heart and stamina, with a good disposition too. It seemed that everyone who saw him, whites and Indians alike, had something good to say. I'd already had several handsome offers for him and turned them all down. I'd also refused a couple of generous trades from Indians who had hoped to make him theirs. I kept him locked in the barn at night because I wasn't interested in parting with him.

The baby laughed out loud, and the Indian's brow lowered in anger before he whipped his head around to glare at his family. The woman curved her arm around the baby and turned her shoulder toward the brave, as though to shield the child from harm.

The Indian turned back to me while the woman bounced the baby in her arms, her eyes flitting between the brave and the child. I saw her pull out a ball of red cloth and hold it out for her child to take. The child grabbed the ball in one hand and then raised its face toward its mother. The baby grinned, its dark eyes dancing, and then it lifted its little hand and patted the woman's cheek.

"Fine horse," the brave said again. "You trade?"

My eyes still watching the child's antics, I thought I would honor the Indian by paying his family a compliment. "I'll trade for that baby," I said.

The Indian gave a single nod of his head. "Good," he said. "Fair trade." He turned and strode away from me, toward the woman, who shrank back from him, clutching the baby to her chest.

"No," I called. "I didn't mean it."

The Indian ignored me. He grabbed the child around its middle and pulled it away from its mother.

The cry that rose from the woman's throat cut my heart in two and made my blood run cold. The Indian was on his way back to the fence, dangling the baby in front of him.

"You take," the Indian said, holding the baby out.

I put my hands up to ward off the child. "No. I don't want to take the baby."

The Indian's face grew dark with anger.

I could see that I had made a terrible mistake in thinking that the Indian could take a joke, and I couldn't think of any way out of it. I didn't know how to tell the man that I had only been teasing, but my attempt at a compliment had broken a mother's heart and made me feel sick clear down through my soul.

I'd had this awful feeling once before, when I had let Jake Anders finally talk me into selling him my big black stallion for a handsome sum. For two nights I couldn't sleep worth a pan of beans. The money was no comfort because all I could think about was my horse. Finally, I approached Jake and told him that

I'd made a terrible mistake. It took twice the purchase price to get my stallion back, but he was worth every penny.

Well, because I had made this blunder with the Indian, albeit unwittingly, I had to set it right. Even though I figured my horse was lost for good—a fact that made my heart sink like a stone in a cold-water pond—at least I could make amends to the baby's mother.

"You," I began, swallowing the lump in my throat. "You can have the horse."

The Indian's face cleared, and he pushed the child up against my chest with such force that I nearly stumbled backward. I instinctively grabbed the child to keep my balance and to keep it from falling. The chilling wails of the baby's mother sent shivers up my spine, even though it was a warm day.

The Indian let himself into the corral and pulled the lead rope out of my hand, his eyes shining as he looked over his new possession. My insides caved when I saw the Indian with my young stallion, but worse than that was the torture of having to listen to the mother weep for her baby.

"Take the stallion," I said. The Indian headed for the open gate.

"And take the baby," I called, holding the child out toward him. "You can have them both."

The Indian stopped short, forcing the stallion to dig his hooves into the dirt in order to keep from running his new master down. The Indian glared at me. "Girl child yours," he spat in a voice so venomous that it stopped me cold. Something in his eyes sealed up my mouth and curbed any further protests. It would be a mistake to invoke this man's wrath. I was sure there would be a fierce price to pay, one that might be taken out on my family or even his own. I feared that the child in my arms would suffer if I insisted that she return home with her parents.

I couldn't understand the Indian's attitude. I knew that sons were more highly valued in Indian camps than daughters, but she was his child, after all. Perhaps he would lose respect in his tribe if he did not honor the terms of the trade that he had agreed to.

The Indian drew himself up to his full height and said, "When me trade, me trade."

Then he turned and stalked toward his woman. He gave her a sharp command and she fell into step behind him, her face buried in her hands as her shoulders shaking with sobs.

I wished I could tell her that I would take good care of her baby. I wished with all my heart that I could let her know that we would treat her like one of our own.

I stared after the retreating couple, paralyzed, until a touch as soft as a butterfly wing brushed against my chin. Startled, I looked down to find a little pair of black eyes staring up at me, a little brown hand patting my face. Then the baby turned her little pink mouth up into a grin.

I smiled back, even though my heart ached for the child's mother. Then I turned toward the house. It was time to introduce my wife to our new daughter.

Somewhere around 1860, Daniel Henrie had a promising young horse that was envied by white men and Indians alike. One day an Indian and his wife came to the Henrie house and asked about trading for the horse. Daniel was in a jovial mood and teased that he would trade his horse for the Indian baby the woman held in her arms. He was horrified when the Indian brave pulled the baby away from her mother and placed her in Daniel's arms.

Daniel tried to give the baby back, insisting that the Indian could keep both the horse and the baby, but it's reported that the Indian refused with the words, "When me trade, me trade." The Indian left with the horse, his weeping wife at his side.

Earlier in his life, Daniel Henrie had let a friend of his talk him into selling his favorite black stallion. Afterward, Daniel was so distraught that he couldn't sleep. He ended up buying the stallion back for twice the amount he'd sold it for.

Source: *Saga of the Sanpitch* 7 (1975): 1

A Rude Welcome

I cut the dough with a floured glass, and then laid the circles out on a tin sheet. I peeked inside the oven to see a pan full of biscuits browned to perfection. I pulled them out and set the hot pan onto the wooden sideboard. Then I slipped the last pan of doughy biscuits inside and closed the oven door.

Even though there were far too many biscuits for me to eat myself, I liked to bake ahead. The oven made the house so hot, that unless it was the dead of winter, I tried to get as much baking done in one day as I could.

I shot a calculating look at the overflowing cookie jar—enough cookies. Maybe I should mix and bake a cake too. I debated about the extra work it would take as I lifted the lid off the big pot of stew on the stove. Earl wasn't going to be back from his coal run tonight. I'd be lucky if he even showed up by tomorrow, though I certainly hoped he would. The big pot of stew would take care of our supper for a couple of days at least, and it was always better the day after I made it.

With the last of the biscuit dough in the oven, I swept the table clean of flour, and wiped my hands on my apron. They were still sticky with dough so I dipped them into the tin pan of wash water. I'd used the same water all day long to wash up the dishes, and it had turned cold. Since it left a greasy sheen on my hands when I pulled them out, I decided it was useless to try to clean anything else with it.

I wiped my hands on my apron and picked up the wash pan. I knew that I really should carry it out into the yard and pour the used water on the garden, but I was too impatient to walk clear out there. My mind was fixed on mixing a cake before the oven cooled down too much to get it baked.

I carried wash water across the door, pulled the door open, and flung the water out. Before it had even left the pan, I desperately wished I could call it back. But it was too late; I could only stare in horror as the water flew smack into the face of a broad-shouldered Indian man. His eyes widened in shocked surprise and then narrowed with anger as he glared at me.

"Oh, oh, I'm so sorry," I gasped.

The Indian spat some words at me that I didn't understand, but I didn't need an interpreter to be certain that what he was saying was uncomplimentary. He raised a dark hand and rubbed it across his forehead.

"I didn't know you were there," I said. I couldn't tell whether he understood English or not, but I had to at least try to explain that I hadn't seen him coming, and that I didn't mean any disrespect.

"Please, come in and get dry," I said.

I wouldn't normally invite an Indian inside with my husband gone, but this was not a normal circumstance. I had to appease this Indian before he got angry enough to retaliate. I was just glad that my children were having their afternoon naps in the other room and that the door was closed.

The Indian strode inside. I had intended for my invitation to put him in a better frame of mind, but instead his scowl deepened.

I pulled out a chair. "Sit down," I said. I turned to the wooden towel bar next to the sink and pulled a towel off it. I spun around to pat the man's face with the towel, trying to dry him off. He snatched the towel from me and wiped it across his face himself, but his scowl remained.

What else could I do? I spied the pan of biscuits cooling on the sideboard. Perhaps some bread would help his mood. I stacked some biscuits in my hand and slid them onto a plate.

"Here," I said, setting the plate on the table. He looked down at the biscuits and then up at me. He grunted, picked up a biscuit, and bit into it. His frown remained.

Maybe the biscuits were too dry. I'd made them to go with soup, and I hadn't given him any butter. If I did, would he even know what to do with it? Maybe he'd eat it plain.

I turned, lifted the coffeepot, poured a cup, and set it on the table before him. The Indian picked up the cup and raised it to his mouth. I hoped it wasn't too hot. He drank the coffee with his scowl firmly in place, so I pulled a handful of cookies out of the cookie jar and laid them next to the biscuits on his plate for good measure.

The Indian picked up a cookie and turned it over and over in his hand. Then he sniffed it and took a bite, his eyes on me. He chewed, and his brow cleared for the first time since I'd laid eyes on him. He stuffed the rest of the cookie in his mouth and grabbed another.

By the time the Indian was satisfied, the cookie jar was half empty, but it was a small price to pay for my family's safety.

Without a word, the Indian stood up. He grabbed a handful of cookies and strode out the door. I collapsed against the table. I hadn't realized how tense I'd been until he was gone.

"Mama?" Leo stood in the bedroom doorway, his hair sticking up on one side.

"Leo!" I hurried over to my little boy. "Are you all right?"

Leo looked up at me with heavy-lidded eyes. "Can I have a cookie?"

I laughed in relief. "Of course! You can have two! Just eat your supper first."

Amy called out from inside the bedroom. "Mama?"

I brought my daughter to the table and fed my children biscuits and stew. After they finished, I let them have as many cookies as they wanted.

Little Amy crumbled a cookie in her small fist and tried to push the crumbs in her mouth. I laughed and picked her up in my arms. I carried her out to do chores and Leo followed along behind.

A bay horse trotted over to the fence to meet us.

"Hi, Donkey!" Leo called out to the old horse.

I wondered if my children would forever be confused about donkeys and horses because when I was a child I couldn't tell the difference between any animals with four legs, hooves, and a tail. The first time I called our new colt a donkey, my older brother thought it was hilarious, and the name stuck. When I got married and moved out of the house, Donkey came with me.

I stepped into the paddock and lifted Amy onto Donkey's back. Leo clamored for his turn. It felt good to stand next to the warm comfort of my old horse. Donkey followed us inside the barn and waited while we milked the cow. He watched us scatter grain for the chickens, and I pretended not to see Leo give Donkey a handful of chicken feed to eat. Even though we stayed out in the paddock for longer than usual, Donkey didn't want us to leave. He must have been missing the horses that Earl had taken with him to pull the coal wagon.

"I'm lonely too," I said, rubbing Donkey's forehead. "But don't worry. They should all be back tomorrow."

Finally the sun lowered enough that I had to tell the children that it was time to tell Donkey good night. We made sure he had plenty of hay and water before we made our way back to the house.

I locked the door and got the children ready for bed.

"When's Papa coming home?" Leo asked.

"He should be back tomorrow, I hope."

"He's been gone a long time," Leo said, looking out the window.

"Only two days."

"Why did he have to go?"

"To get coal for us to burn in the winter to keep warm."

"So after I sleep and wake up he'll be here?"

"No, it will be later in the day—at nighttime," I said. *Unless he has a broken wagon wheel, or a lame horse, or runs into unfriendly Indians.* I kept my thoughts to myself, but I couldn't keep from shuddering.

"Mama, are you cold?" Leo asked. "Should I build you a fire?"

"No, thank you, Leo!"

The house was still plenty warm from the baking earlier in the day. I hoped that I'd fed the Indian enough cookies to make him forget my accidental insult of splashing dirty water on him. An Indian with a grudge was a dangerous thing; they tended to strike first and never ask questions later.

"Tell me a story," Leo begged.

I told my children stories until they drifted off to sleep—Leo with his ruddy cheek pressed into the pillow and Amy with her thumb in her mouth.

I got up from beside my sleeping children and moved into the kitchen, ready to put myself to bed too. Once I was asleep, the time would pass more quickly and it would be that much closer to the time when Earl would be home.

As soon as I stepped out of the bedroom, the front doorknob rattled. Fear shot up my spine. I whipped my head around to stare at the door, grabbing the back of a chair so that my knees wouldn't collapse. The knob was quiet and still.

Had I really heard something? My heart pounded hard enough to assure me that I had. It wasn't my imagination; someone was trying to get in.

With my eyes still fixed on the knob, it rattled again. I jumped as if it were a striking snake. I threw an anxious glance toward the room where my children lay sleeping. Knowing that I was their sole source of protection forced my courage to the surface.

My eyes darted around the room, looking for something—anything—that I could use as a weapon. The knob rattled again with such force that the door thumped inside its casing. I clutched at my throat, trying to keep my fear from erupting into a scream. My eyes fell on the poker standing by the fireplace. I dashed across the floor and grabbed it. I wished that it were red-hot, but I had to settle for room temperature.

I flattened myself against the wall and walked on cat feet toward the door. I wondered if the sound of my voice would frighten whoever was on the other side of the door away.

Impatient feet stamped outside, and the doorknob shook

again. This time I was so close that I was startled into nearly dropping the poker.

"Who's there?" I called. My throat was so dry that the words got stuck and came out as a whisper.

In reply, there was more stamping and a low chuckle. What if there was a drunken Indian waiting outside? How could I possibly reason with him?

The door rattled in its frame again. Whoever was out there wasn't going to give up and go away.

"I have a weapon," I called out.

The doorknob rattled.

I had to get rid of whoever it was before they thought of setting the house on fire or something equally horrifying. I reached out toward the knob, my fear as sharp as an axe. I worked the lock loose with quiet fingers and gripped the doorknob as I hefted the poker in my other hand. I would wait for the next rattle—wait for whoever it was to try the door again—so that they wouldn't be expecting me to fling the door open and smack them with the poker.

The doorknob jiggled. I gave it a fierce twist, pulling the door open and raising the poker at the same time.

Donkey gave a snort of surprise and stepped back, his eyes wide.

"Donkey!" I cried, my voice coming out in a sob. I lowered the poker and sagged in relief against the horse's side. "Oh, Donkey, I thought you were an Indian coming to murder me!"

Donkey chuckled a soft whinny and nuzzled my shoulder.

"How did you get out of your pen?" I asked with mock severity. "You're not allowed to sleep in the house, you know, but I'm awfully glad you're here, just the same."

I stroked Donkey's nose. "Come on, I'll go tuck you in next to the cow so you won't be lonely." I pulled Donkey toward the barn and he followed willingly. "I'll even tell you a bedtime story about a lady who accidentally threw her wash water onto an Indian."

Sometime in the 1880s, Elizabeth finished mixing bread and set it to raise. She washed her hands in the tin washbasin and tossed the water out the door, right into the face of an Indian brave. He was very angry and was only pacified when Elizabeth's sister Johanna offered him a plate of cookies and coffee.

Ann was home alone with her children while her husband was gone overnight to get a load of coal. In the evening, the doorknob rattled, and Ann was afraid it might be hostile Indians. She armed herself with a poker, just in case, and opened the door to find the lone horse that had been left behind (which I named Donkey), looking for company.

In none of my research did I come up with last names for any of these ladies. In the interest of storytelling, I combined the stories into one.

Source: *Saga of the Sanpitch* 17 (1985), 98.

One Against

"They can't get away with it," To-ko-witz growled. "We must not let them think that the battle is won."

"I agree," said Mon-dats. "We need white blood."

I didn't say anything, even though I wanted to remind Mon-dats that the blood of the white-skinned people had proven to run as red as ours when it spilled from their bodies. It's true that it made a brighter contrast against their pale skin, especially if their hair was the strange, ghost color of many spiderwebs strung together over their heads. It was fascinating, this light color that made me think they already had half of their spirit in the grave. The spider hair made them look old, even if their faces were young. I wondered if these light-hairs felt the wounds of death as keenly as those of us with the solid skin color of earth. I had killed my share of the pale skins, but I hadn't known how to ask them how it felt to die.

"We'll lie in ambush," To-ko-witz said. "Many of the pale skins are coming into the canyon to cut wood."

"Bah," said Orro-kani with disgust. "They build their shelters thick and solid, and they don't move them with the seasons. They squat together like ants crawling over a carcass, and their dwellings are as ugly as a pile of moose turds."

This made me laugh. It was so like Orro-kani to speak his mind. Even though he was one who liked to laugh, I would not want to be on the wrong end of the spear if Orro-kani were my enemy. There would be nothing left of me if he truly wanted to be rid of me. He was the fiercest warrior I knew.

"They make good bread," I mumbled. My stomach growled in agreement. The others stared at me, their eyes narrowed.

"What?" I asked.

"You would trade a loaf of bread for the lands of your forefathers?" To-ko-witz demanded.

"No, of course not." I set my jaw so they would not ask me any more questions. Was I the only one who missed the days when the white settlers first came to our valley? They had come here during a time of first cold, bringing their fat cattle, who were so tame that they stood and watched while you notched your arrow and let it fly toward their hearts. Then they would fall over dead. They were more accommodating than deer or elk. As the winter wore on and the snow piled deep, the cattle began to die of their own accord. We would drag off their carcasses and feast in our camp.

More settlers came the next year, bringing more cattle. We found it to be much more convenient to drive the cattle into the mountains before slaughtering them because some of the settlers didn't like us to help ourselves. They had a strange word—stealing. We didn't have such a word in our language. We saw things very differently from the whites, with their pale eyes. We took what we needed, and we took what we wanted. If anyone could take it back from us, then it was theirs by rights and they deserved to have it more than we did.

We soon discovered that some of the cows gave milk and cream, and the that whites had magical machines that turned cream into butter and buttermilk. I had even been to Walter Cox's house on some occasions when they had made ice cream. They shared it with me, as they did their other food. When I lifted a spoonful of ice cream to my tongue, it hurt. I yanked the spoon away, thinking I'd been burned. But the little Cox children were putting spoonful after spoonful into their mouths. The bit of ice cream on my tongue melted and I caught the flavor. I had never had anything like it before. I thought that it must be the food of the Gods. I scooped the rest of my ice cream into my mouth as quickly as the awkward spoon would allow. When Walter's missus saw my empty bowl, she looked into my eyes, smiled, and served me more ice cream.

"Mama," said one of her daughters, called E-mi-lee. "May I have more?"

"No, I'm sorry. There is no more."

E-mi-lee stuck out her bottom lip. "Then why does he get more?" She pointed her spoon at me, and I began to scoop the ice cream into my mouth faster.

"He's our guest," said Missus Cox.

I grinned at E-mi-lee and opened my mouth wide to take in the last bite of ice cream, delighting in the shock of cold that melted into sweetness that surpassed any of the berries or honey that I'd ever found in the forest.

E-mi-lee wasn't a spiderweb hair but her sister Sarah was. When Sarah saw that my bowl was empty, she leaned over to take it from me. I reached up to touch her hair. She jerked away, a look of surprise in her strange round eyes, which were as blue as the sky in summer. I wondered if everything looked blue through her sky eyes.

"It's all right, Sarah," said Cox. "He's not used to blonde hair, that's all."

Sarah gave me a thin smile and hurried into the kitchen with my bowl.

I burped as loudly as I could so that Missus Cox would know how much I liked the food she'd given me, especially the ice cream. E-mi-lee gasped and put her hand over her mouth as though she'd burned her tongue on a roasted cricket. One of the little Cox boys laughed out loud, and I grinned at him.

Nearly all of the whites would give us food when we asked. Most of them handed it to us through half-opened doors, which they then shut it in our faces instead of inviting us to eat with them like Cox did.

There was one white woman, the crazy Yew-nees Warner, who held no good will toward us, even though her husband had honor in death by killing an Indian before he'd been killed. It was an even exchange—a trade that balanced the numbers in the best possible proportions. Yet Yew-nees didn't seem satisfied that her husband had died a noble warrior's death and gone to the best afterlife—

one far better than if he'd died an old man in his wigwam.

I had gone along when we'd been to visit Yew-nees at the dwelling of her parents after we'd made peace from the killings. Her father was a white leader, a man we called "Captain." He was reasonable about war. He knew that it was simply a way of life; once their deaths were avenged, there was no sense in hanging onto the dead with a heavy heart.

One of those who had killed Warner claimed his strange neck cloth, although he didn't tie it in the same fashion as Warner had, with a knot that slid magically along the length of fabric. Warner also had some curious talismans with him, including a metal cylinder from which folded out some of the most wondrous tools that we had ever seen. None of us had been selfish; we broke several of the tools off so that we might all share in the new and wonderful things that the pale skins brought with them. Yet, when we visited as guests in Yew-nees's home, she glared at us as if we were demons. My fellow warrior adjusted his neck cloth and smiled at her, thinking that if she saw how we honored her husband's belongings, it would prove to her that we held him in the highest regard.

We all pulled out the pieces of metal that we had divided between us and laid them out on the table for her to see with what honor we esteemed the brave Warner.

As soon as she saw the items, a most wondrous change occurred in Yew-nees's face—it drained of what little color it had until she truly appeared as one dead. Her eyes narrowed and her mouth compressed into a thin line. She hardly looked human anymore. Even though she was obviously with child, she wasn't slow to grab up a knife and start toward us. If she had reached us, I have no doubt that she would have done her best to plunge the blade into at least one of us, possibly more, since we were so surprised at her actions. Yet she didn't get the chance to kill even one of us. Instead, her father grabbed her by the shoulders and pulled her from the room. A sound escaped her mouth—a strangled cry that didn't even sound human.

We laughed in amazement at her power and determination.

She would have a strong papoose, of that we were all in complete agreement.

Captain returned alone. If he had beaten her while in the other room in order to teach her to keep her place, she hadn't cried out—not even once. Our admiration for her grew, as well as our conviction that she was possessed of an unusual spirit.

It was after she had her papoose that one of our young men, Enapay, who had heard our stories of Yew-nees decided to go and ask for bread from her household. He said he wanted to see this pale devil woman. He would have to go without me because I remembered, all too well, the knife that had come for me faster than I had thought possible.

We could see the fort from our Indian camp. We watched Enapay go in and, later, we saw him come running out, screaming and crying that the devil woman had beaten him nearly dead. When he calmed down enough to make sense, he said that he had found her alone with her papoose. He asked for bread.

"No." she said. "Go away."

She was not a large woman, or tall. Enapay closed the door and leaned against it. "Give me bread," he said. He was determined not to be put off by this small white woman. He would make her do as he commanded, as a woman should.

Yew-neese laid her papoose down on the bed. "That baby stared at me with its strange, pale eyes," Enapay said, his own eyes growing wide with the memory. "He bewitched me and fixed me to my spot. I couldn't move. Then Yew-nees pulled a stick from where it propped up one of their glass walls. The pane of glass crashed down, sounding just like rifle fire. I thought that someone was shooting outside, so my attention was distracted. Then she came at me with her stick, swinging it with such ferocity that I didn't even have time to pull my blanket up around my shoulders to protect myself. She beat me until I had to cry for mercy or die. At last that devil-woman opened her door and told me to get out."

Enapay showed us the bruises and bloody cuts on his back and shoulders.

When Chief Arropeen heard his tale, he told Enapay that he deserved just what he got.

"I was bewitched!" Enapay declared.

"Squaw," Arropeen said.

Ever since that exchange, Enapay had been "Squaw," and not one of us would ever ask Yew-neese for anything. Sometimes the children of our tribe would dare each other to approach her and touch her skirt, but it was a rare child who would even take up the challenge, and none followed through. Yew-neese was possessed of a devil spirit, there was no doubt about that, but we still called Enapay "Squaw."

The Cox family was as opposite of Yew-nees as it was possible to be. They would always smile when they saw that it was me at their door. They invited me in, cut the bread thick, and spread it with some of their good, sweet butter before handing over it to me. Sometimes it had golden honey poured over it, if they had any. They would ask me to sit at their own table to eat, bringing a cold glass of milk for me to drink with the bread. I felt as though I was one of their tribe.

If all whites had been like that, more of them would have kept their hair Yet some whites called us names, cheated us in trading, and taught their children to throw rocks at our children.

Recently, some of our tribe had been killed in a skirmish a day's ride south. We had to avenge our tribesmen, and we now sought enemy blood.

"We will kill some of the men who are cutting down our trees in the canyon," Mon-dats declared.

"They always have some of their numbers stand guard with fire sticks," said To-ko-witz.

"We'll get them first," said Orro-kani. "We'll gather enough of us to kill the fire-stick holders, and then we'll kill the rest." His eyes shone with eagerness.

"Or we could lie in wait and ambush anyone going into the canyon," I said. "They won't be expecting us to wait patiently. They think we're blood-thirsty barbarians."

Orro-kani turned his eyes to me. "We could be as sneaky as

rabbits in a burrow," he said. I thought he was poking fun at me, until he said, "We could be rabbits hiding the teeth of a bear in our mouths and the claws of a cougar in our paws!" He grinned, and I grinned back.

"Are we all agreed to this plan?" To-ko-witz asked. He looked at each of us in turn, and we all gave him a nod of assent.

"All agree," he announced. "Let's go spill some paleface blood and avenge our brothers."

"The first ones to come along," Mon-dats said. "We'll kill them before they can even scream."

My heart pounded with anticipation as we grabbed our weapons and headed for the canyon mouth. I even let myself hope that maybe there would be a flame-hair among those who would fall into our trap. I had seen only two flame-hairs in my life, and I would be proud to own a scalp like that. It couldn't help but bring me luck, to have a scalp with such powerful magic as to be the color of fire.

We made our way through the trees along the river that ran along the bottom of the canyon. When I spotted the white man's bridge, I had an idea. "Wait!" I said. "Let's hide under the bridge. It will be the perfect place to wait for our victims. After they've crossed, we'll attack from behind and they won't even see us coming."

Orro-kani placed a firm hand on my shoulder. "Good thinking," he said. "I say we make our burrow under the path that spans the river."

Again, To-ko-witz checked that we were all in agreement, and then he led the way to the bridge. We hunkered beneath it, weapons in hand, our heads tilted upward to listen for any sound of feet on the planks of wood that stretched out into a shelter over our heads.

We were patient. After a time, we heard the sounds of female voices and laughter.

It was difficult to keep my heart calm as the voices grew louder and the sound of feet rattled the boards over our heads. Females had long hair, and long hair made the best scalps. It sounded as if there could be one for each of us. I strained to hear the sound of a male voice, but none came to my ears. It was rare to have women pale-skins out alone—stupid women. Even if they had a firestick, we would be upon them before they could raise it toward us.

After the feet left the bridge, To-ko-witz signaled to us. We slid like shadows into the brush beside the road to make our attack.

Six white women walked along the road ahead, baskets in their hands. I grinned. After the massacre, we could take the baskets, which surely carried food for the pale men cutting trees in our mountains.

So much the better. If we took the lives of women who belonged to the men, they would be wounded in their hearts as well. Even better than that, we would get some white men's food to eat.

I was suddenly hungry. Their bread was so fine compared to the fry cakes made from coarse flour that our women ground with rocks. Too bad for the pale men gathering wood. They would now have to do without food and without women.

Then my eyes stopped on a head of hair the color of spiderwebs. Many whites had light hair of different shades, but something about this hair struck a memory in me. When the smaller woman beside her turned to say something to spider-silk hair, I nearly gasped out loud—it was the face of E-mi-lee, Cox's daughter. And spiderweb hair was Sarah. I knew it without having to see her face.

"Stop!" I hissed.

Orro-kani spun around and scowled at me.

"We cannot do this," I said.

"Why?" Orro-kani demanded. His eyes narrowed into angry slits, his fist wrapped around the shaft of his bow, and his fingers worked the fletching on his arrow.

"I know those women," I said.

"Then you get to kill the ones you know," Orro-kani said.

"No. I cannot kill them. They are daughters of my friend."

"Whites are not our friends," Orro-kani spat. "That's why we're doing this." He shook his head as though despairing of my sanity.

"We must vote," To-ko-witz said. "Who is ready to kill these white maggots and get them off our land?"

Orro-kani nodded his head, and so did the others. I shook my head no.

Orro-kani looked at me as if he would like to kill me.

"We have one against," To-ko-witz announced, not sounding the least bit happy about it. "It is over."

Orro-kani gave a gasp of disappointment loud enough that I was sure the women would hear him. I glanced down the road where the white women were disappearing around the bend. Not one of them looked back.

"You rabbit!" Orro-kani snapped. He stomped off through the forest. I knew his feet were heavier than they needed to be.

A couple of weeks later, I went looking for Cox and found him in his field. As soon as he saw me, his face broke into a smile as broad as the yoke he had on his oxen's shoulders. He showed no sign of fear, even though I had my bow in my hand and a quiver full of arrows slung across my back. "Are you hungry?" Cox asked. "Come, share my lunch," he said. He didn't even hesitate, and I knew I had done right in sparing his daughter's lives, even though I was about as popular in camp as a bloated buzzard.

Cox opened his cloth bag and pulled out some bread and a lump of yellow that he called cheese. It was soft, chewy, and salty, and it tasted delicious.

"Cox," I said, "Don't let your E-mi-lee and Sarah go in the mountains alone any more."

His eyes opened wide in surprise. "Why? What's wrong?"

"They could get dead."

Cox's face darkened. "Is this a threat? Haven't I always been your friend?"

I held up one hand to ward off his sudden anger. I had enough people mad at me back in camp. "It is because you are my friend that your daughters are alive," I said. I told him of our plans, and how I had voted against the massacre.

Cox's eyes got wet, just like a woman's. I looked away so I wouldn't have to see his loss of manhood dripping down his face.

"You are a true friend," he said, his voice tight and garbled with women's water. I was feeling sorry that I had told him anything. Certainly women were valuable property but not worth crying over. Cox's his next words redeemed him in my eyes.

"Come to my house tonight," he said. "Come and have all the ice cream you can eat."

Around 1864, Jane Reid, Christena Anderson, Susan Henrie, Liz Johnson, and Sarah and Emily Cox wanted to visit their sweethearts, who were spending the summer cutting timber up in the mountains. Since there had been a month with no hostile Indian activity, their parents agreed to let the girls go. The visit to the timber camp and back was accomplished without any problems.

A few days later, it was learned that a group if Indians had been hiding under a bridge in the canyon on the day the girls made their journey, intent on killing the first whites they saw. The only reason the girls were spared is that one of the Indians in the group was friends with Sarah and Emily's father, Frederick Walter Cox, and recognized the girls. All Indians had to be in agreement for a massacre to be carried out, but this Indian voted no.

Eunice Warner Snow wrote a firsthand account of her troubles with the Indians. On October 4, 1853, she was pregnant with her first child when her husband, John, and his companion, William Mills, were killed by Indians while tending the grist mill at the mouth of Manti Canyon. After the Indians made peace, they said that Eunice's husband had fought desperately, managing to kill an Indian. One wore her husband's necktie on his bare neck, and they showed her his slide rule and penknife, from which they had broken off the ear spoon and button hook.

Once an Indian man came asking Eunice for bread. He wouldn't leave when she told him to, so she beat him with a stick until he cried like a baby. Arropeen said it served him right, and all the Indians called him "squaw" after that. "Squaw" was a more derogatory term than simply calling him a woman.

Source: Eunice Warner Snow, "A Short Accounting of Troubles and Trials with the Indians," in *Saga of the Sanpitch* 16 (1984): 30; 29 (1997): 41.

Is The Doctor in?

An urgent knock sounded at the door. I pushed the cork into a newly filled bottle of cough medicine, set it down, and then hurried to the door, hoping that whoever was on the other side wasn't seriously ill or hurt. My husband was the doctor, not me. Whoever was waiting would have to come back later. Babies have their own timetable, and because my husband was out on a birthing call, I couldn't guess when he'd be home.

I grabbed the handle and pulled the door open. It was worse than I thought. I gasped and took a step back, my eyes widening at the sight of a tall Indian named Brockley standing in the doorway. He didn't smile; in fact, he didn't seem pleased to see me at all. His eyes darted around the interior of the clinic before he jabbed a dark finger at the sign hanging outside. It read, "Teeth extracted with pleasure, without pain, without price."

My heart did a little hop-skip of dread. I hoped against hope that Brockley hadn't come for a tooth extraction. If my husband tried to pull a tooth from this Indian's mouth, I was afraid that Brockley would bite down hard enough to take off one of Joe's fingers. "Dr. Nine-fingers" didn't sound nearly as good as "Dr. Richards."

"White medicine here?" Brockley asked, taking two steps inside but leaving the door open.

I was pretty sure that he meant the white medicine man, so I answered, "No."

"My baby sick," Brockley said. He folded his arms and scowled. "My son need white medicine now. Medicine man no good."

"What's wrong with him?"

"He call on spirits, he shake sacred rattles, and they not listen. Spirits angry."

I nodded as though I'd meant that my question was about the tribal medicine man all along. I wasn't going to be the one to tell Brockley that I'd really been asking about his son.

"And what seems to be the matter with your son?" I asked, making sure there would be no misunderstanding this time.

There was a shift in Brockley's countenance—a hardening around his eyes.

"What illness does he have?" I asked, hoping to correct any faux pas I may have committed.

Brockley folded his arms and narrowed his eyes at me. "He cough all time, *kugh, kugh.*" He demonstrated with a fake cough of his own.

I nodded. "Anything else?"

"He no breath nose." Brockley shoved two fingers up his nostrils. "Clogged."

I nodded again.

"Him spot here, there, all place." Brockley tapped his fingers in various places all over his cheeks and forehead.

"I think I have something that will help," I said. I stepped over to the bottles lined up in the cupboard and scanned the labels before selecting one. I turned and held it out toward Brockley. "Here."

When he reached for it, I instinctively pulled back a little. I slipped the bottle through my fingers until I held it by the neck in between my thumb and forefinger.

Brockley snatched the bottle with a "humph" of disgust. I could have shown more disgust than that at the fingers he'd had up his nose, but I practiced restraint.

"What is?" Brockley asked, holding the bottle close to his eyes, trying to see through the brown glass.

"Medicine."

Brockley gave me a blank look.

"Give some to your son," I said, and pointed my finger into my mouth.

"Eat?" he asked.

"Yes." I pointed my finger into my mouth again. "He eat medicine." I pointed to the bottle.

Brockley nodded, turned away from me, and headed toward the Indian camp that was a short distance from the fort.

I went back to my task of pouring cough syrup into bottles. I was nearly done when I heard a shout from outside. It sounded as though someone was quite upset about something.

I stepped to the front of the clinic and glanced out the window. What I saw sent a ripple of terror from my head to my feet. Brockley charged straight toward me, a large knife in his hand and murder in his eyes. Something was terribly wrong.

He would be certain to blame me if his child happened to die right after he gave him the medicine I'd put in his hand. He wouldn't wait for explanations either, and I wasn't going to stay and hope that he might ask for one.

I dropped the medicine bottle that I held, heedless of the dark syrup the spilled out onto the floor. My life was worth more than a bottle of cough medicine.

I picked up my skirts and dashed for the back door. I flung it open and darted outside. As I sped down the alley, I heard the front door of the clinic bang open. A crash of glass only served to spur my feet to greater speed. A roar from Brockley's throat sent me flying even faster, my skirt flapping like wings.

I had to get off the street, or else Brockley would spot me and get me for sure. Even while I was running for my life, I had no doubt that Brockley could throw his knife with enough accuracy to hit me squarely in the back. The muscles around my spine tensed and twitched at the very thought. As much as he might love me, my husband didn't possess enough medical magic to repair what would surely be a mortal wound at the hand of a well-muscled Indian fueled by rage. Even if Brockley didn't manage to hit any vital organs, a wound with the knife gripped in his fist would surely cause me to bleed to death in a matter of minutes.

Without stopping to knock, I wrenched open Eunice Brown's door and ducked inside. A bellow of primitive fury sounded from the street outside. I slammed the door shut. Eunice looked up from her potato peeling, her eyes wide with amazement. If Brockley had seen me come in here, I was dead. Perhaps Eunice was too.

"Help me," I begged, my eyes filling with tears. "Please, for the love of God, hide me!"

Without wasting time on questions, Eunice's eyes darted to the spot where the quilt on her bed touched the floor. Then she swept her gaze across the row of clothes hanging on pegs along the wall. She stabbed the potato she held with her paring knife—an uncomfortable reminder of what Brockley intended to do to me. Then Eunice stood and crossed the room, opening the door that led to the lean-to built on the back of her house. "In here."

I darted toward Eunice like a moth to a lantern. As I ran past her, she grabbed my arm and flung me into the space behind the door.

"Stand here," she said, her forehead creased with intensity. "Stay here." She stared at me, and I nodded.

Eunice pushed the door against the wall, trapping me in the little triangle of space next to the door's hinges. She swung a chair up against the edge of the door, a fragile lock to my prison. I watched through the small crack between the door and the wall as Eunice sat down on her stool again and took up her potato and paring knife. She had just pulled the knife out of the partially skinned potato when Brockley burst in through the door.

My knees nearly gave out under me, and I had to clamp my hand over my mouth to keep from screaming with fear.

Brockley ignored Eunice and yanked the cover off the mattress. He bent over and slashed his knife in the space underneath the bed. Then he straightened and glared around the room. I was sure that he could see me and hear my heart banging against my ribs—but his glittering black eyes swept past my hiding place and fastened on the row of clothes hanging against the wall. He strode over to them and slid the flat of his knife against the entire length of clothing. Then he turned and addressed Eunice.

"Where white woman?" he roared. I was trembling so badly that I feared that he would hear my knees knock and stab me right through the narrow gap that I stared through. *This is a stupid hiding place; I'm practically in plain sight. Why did Eunice put me here? I should have run out of the lean-to when I had the chance.*

I was frightened enough when Brockley asked Eunice my whereabouts, but I was struck nearly numb with terror when I saw her lift her hand with the paring knife extended and point straight to my hiding place. She didn't say a word, but her gaze was on me as she betrayed me to certain death.

My eyes rolled back, and I leaned my head against the wall, sagging against the rough logs, heedless of the bark snagging my dress. I recognized my own symptoms—I was going to faint. Then I was going to die.

I could hear Brockley's heavy breathing as he moved toward me. I prayed that the blackness teasing the edges of my mind would close in swiftly enough that I would be oblivious to the hard bite of the steel blade that was coming for me.

Then a horrible thought struck me: *Oh, please, God, no. Don't let him scalp me before he kills me.*

Brockley's tread was so heavy that I could feel the floorboards bend beneath my feet when he reached the door that separated us. I had no doubt that he was strong enough to plunge the knife right through the wooden door and kill me.

Tears burned my eyes, and I squeezed them shut, not wanting to see my death coming. I waited, trembling, stifling the sobs, although I didn't know why I should bother. It was pure instinct, like an animal hiding in its hole, waiting helplessly as the predator digs ever closer at an alarming rate. I waited to die.

It seemed like years before the door moved away from me. I shrank back against the wall. "No, no, it was an accident," I cried. "It wasn't the medicine, it wasn't my fault. Oh, please, don't kill me."

"He's gone," Eunice said, touching my shoulder.

I jumped at her touch, and my eyes flew open. I glanced

from side to side, searching for my killer. I couldn't see him anywhere.

I stared at Eunice with wide eyes. "Where'd he go?" I whispered.

"He ran right through," she said. "He's outside somewhere."

I grabbed her by both shoulders. "Why did you tell him where I was?" I demanded, shaking her. "Why?"

Eunice's gaze was steady on mine. "I'm an honest woman," she declared. "I answered his question with a gesture. It's not my fault if he misinterpreted it to believe that you had escaped outside through my lean-to."

I didn't know whether I should hug her or hit her.

She made me sit down and gave me some tea to drink. I stayed in hiding at Eunice's until my husband returned. He'd heard all about what happened between me and the disgruntled Brockley. He'd even stopped in to check on Brockley's baby and found him to be sleeping peacefully. The crisis over, Brockley greeted my husband with great cheer. He explained with a laugh that when he first gave his son some of the medicine, the little boy's toes had curled up and changed color. Certain that he was dying, he'd gone after the murderer—me. He wasn't the least apologetic for his behavior. He thought it was great sport. When he couldn't find me anywhere in the settlement, the brush, or the willows along the creek, he'd returned home and found his son much improved.

Even after that, Brockley never thanked me. Whenever I encountered him, he acted as though I didn't even exist. That suited me just fine.

Doctor Richards covered a spectrum of medical ills, and in the 1850s hung up a shingle that read, "Teeth extracted with pleasure, without pain, and without price." He explained that the pleasure was his, the pain was the patient's, and he would perform the operation for free.

One day, Brockley the Indian was disappointed to find the white medicine man out when he came seeking relief for his baby boy, who apparently suffered from measles. Mrs. Richards gave Brockley medicine that turned the boy's toes up. Certain that his son was dying, the enraged Brockley went after Mrs. Richards with a knife. She ran into Eunice Brown's house, where Mrs. Brown hid her behind the lean-to door before resuming her potato peeling.

When Brockley appeared and demanded Mrs. Richard's whereabouts, Mrs. Brown couldn't bring herself to lie. She gestured toward the lean-to door, and Brockley ran through. Eventually he returned home and found his son much improved.

Sources: Ruth Scow (Mrs. Brown's great-granddaughter), *Song of a Century* (Manti, Utah: Utah Centennial Committee, 1949).

A Token of Love

I slid my eyes around the circle of faces surrounding the campfire. Josiah was still not there, and by now, I was fairly sure he wasn't going to show up.

I tried not to care. After all, he was just a trail hand.

I hid a yawn and then pushed myself to my feet. I felt eyes on me, and glanced down to see the Holman brothers staring up at me with undisguised adoration. I tucked a strand of my fox-red hair behind one ear and favored them with a smile. Then my smile slipped and I turned away. I'd trade every stare I ever got from every man for a single kiss from Josiah.

Oh, why did I have to feel this way? My cheeks warmed as my mind filled with thoughts of him. I'd caught his dark eyes on me enough times to know that he was interested. I admit that I'd flirted with him, and found his confident replies, playful banter and proud bearing to be downright intriguing.

I headed for the wagon that I had been assigned to share with the Carson family. Their four little boys looked so much alike that I never could keep their names straight, and Emily Carson, the mother of the brood, was in constant need of my help. If I'd wanted to be a mother, I'd had plenty of marriage offers already. I turned them all down for good reasons. Those men were the same bratty boys who'd teased me mercilessly when I was a skinny, pale-as-milk girl with bright red hair. Now it was my turn to tease them with porcelain skin, green eyes, and dark red tresses that drew them like a siren song.

I looked up at the crescent moon hanging low in the sky. Josiah's earlier warning that no one should ever leave the circle of wagons at night without a guard was positively suffocating. I wanted to walk out into the moonlit night and be by myself.

A strong hand took hold of my arm. I whirled to face my attacker. Josiah grinned down at me, his bronze skin even darker in the night—a perfect backdrop for his arresting white smile. My heart melted, but I didn't let on. I planted one fist on my hip, tilted my chin up, and said, "Unhand me."

Josiah's grin faded, and he let go of my arm. Had I sounded too harsh? He had startled me, but I didn't intend to put him off.

"Sorry, Olivia, but you know you aren't allowed out beyond the wagons after dark without a guard."

I raised one hand to twist a strand of sunset-red hair around my finger. I looked up into Josiah's eyes and asked, "What if I was just wishing on a star?"

"You can do that inside the circle of wagons."

"Well, now that I'm out here, who's going to guard me from the guard?" I nearly laughed out loud at the look on Josiah's face. His eyebrows dipped over his dark eyes and his full mouth twisted ever so slightly underneath his straight nose as he pondered my words. He glanced back over his shoulder, and my heart thudded in appreciation of the sight of his square jaw against the night sky. When he turned back toward me, I glimpsed the dimple in his chin.

Josiah lowered his head, placing it close to mine. "Now, ma'am, that would depend on whether the lady in question wanted guarding or not."

Even in the dim light, I could see Josiah's eyes roving over my face. I hoped he liked what he saw. I turned up the corners of my mouth to make the scenery more pleasant.

"I like to see you smile," Josiah said, his voice husky. "And I'd like to show you something."

My heart caught. "Something I've never seen before?" I teased.

"Not unless you've been through my things." Josiah led the way to the inside of the circle of wagons. I followed him to where his saddlebags rested on the ground. He bent over them and rummaged inside.

I was intrigued. What could he possibly have in there that would be of any interest to me?

Josiah stood and turned toward me with a small silver box in his hand. "It's prettier in the day," he said. "Then the sun lights the scroll work." He lifted the lid, and music spilled out into the night.

I was enchanted. "Oh, that's lovely!"

"It was my mother's."

"It must be very precious," I said.

I could feel Josiah's eyes fastened on me in the silence before he whispered, "It is." Then he stepped in closer, so that the music box was nearly touching us both. I stayed where I was, my face tipped up to Josiah's, my heart thudding an invitation for him to come closer.

"There's something else that's precious to me too," Josiah mumbled.

"And what would that be?" I whispered. I felt a hot stirring inside and my heart grew warm in anticipation. He was going to kiss me at last.

"You." Josiah's lips were so close to my face that his whispered confession felt like the wings of a butterfly against my cheek. I suddenly realized that if he wasn't going to kiss me, then I would surely kiss him.

"Libby!" a small voice lisped.

Josiah pulled away from me and let the music box lid fall closed. My heart sank, and I turned to see one of the little Carson boys, the one who always called me "Libby" instead of "Livvy," pounding his way toward us, .

"Ned said he was gonna bite me and make me bleed!" the little Carson shouted, grabbing my skirt and twisting himself around to make me the shield between him and Ned, who was close on his heels.

"Now, Ned, no more of that," I scolded, shaking my finger as Ned skidded to a stop in front of me.

"But he kicked me in the leg!" Ned said in his own defense. "If he hadn't, I would have caught him by now!"

I turned back to Josiah with an apology on my lips, which was far less satisfying than a kiss. But Josiah had picked up the little Carson and was headed toward our wagon. I followed, herding the grumbling Ned ahead of me. I was grumbling too, but not so anyone could hear.

Josiah deposited the boy into the arms of his father and then moved toward me. I was disappointed that he didn't stop, but he touched my hand as he passed. It was no accident. The brief clasp of his fingers shot sudden warmth up my arm and straight into my heart. "Hope your wish comes true," he said, and then he was gone.

I helped get the boys ready for bed, and fell asleep in my own bedroll beneath the wagon.

I woke up to vibrations in the ground beneath me, drumming a warning through my bones. The distant thunder sounded louder and louder. Was it a stampede?

I raised my head. A storm was headed right for me. The strange thing was, it was coming at me along the ground. When the cloud was so close that I smelled dust, I made out the bodies of horses and riders inside it.

Suddenly, my heart seized my ribs and beat against them so hard that my chest hurt. Dark-skinned men rode those horses, their faces painted in inhuman shades and their straight hair fluttering behind them in black whips that beat against their backs.

I screamed.

One of the smaller Carsons sat up and stared at me with frightened eyes. He scrambled to his feet and tottered away from me, straight toward the Indian riders, his mouth open in a wail that was lost in the thundering hooves and shrieks coming from other wagons.

"No!" I screamed. I untangled myself from my blankets and dashed after the toddler. I scooped him up and turned back to the wagon, bending down to thrust the boy into his mother's outstretched arms.

Then Emily Carson did the strangest thing: her eyes widened in horror and she screamed. Startled, I stepped back. What was wrong with Emily? In the next instant, a strong arm circled my waist and lifted me off my feet.

My mouth opened in angry astonishment. How dare anyone grab me? I gave the arm a hard slap, but it didn't let go. It swung me up and sat me sideways smack in front of an Indian warrior astride his horse.

"Let me go!" I screamed, but the brown arm pulled me in tight, forcing my cheek against a bare brown chest of hot, oily skin stretched over hard muscles. A primitive cry rose from the body, tore the air, and stole my breath away. A shiver of absolute terror ripped through my body.

The brown arm clamped me closer still, so that I could hardly breathe. The horse wheeled and broke into a gallop. The circle of wagons faded into the distance.

"No!" I screamed. I renewed my struggles against the Indian that held me and managed to free one arm. I beat on the Indian's chest with my fist.

The Indian laughed and tightened his grip with his knees on his horse so that both of his hands were free. He grabbed my wrist and laughed again, but there was nothing funny about this to me. His amusement inflamed my anger. I would get free of him now or die trying.

I twisted my face into the Indian's chest, opened my mouth, and struck my teeth into his muscled torso with such force that I blocked my own breathing. I didn't back off, though, not until I had a good grip with my teeth. I bit down with every bit of strength I had, fueled by fear and anger that pounded through me in rhythm with the thud of horse's hooves.

The Indian let out a scream of pain. He turned my wrist loose and grabbed my hair, pulling with all his strength. It felt as if he might rip my head off, but I wouldn't turn him loose. My vision went blurry and I bit down harder. I hoped I was causing him more pain than he was giving me.

Suddenly, the Indian let go of my hair and gave me a sound thump to my head. It hurt, but I still wouldn't let go. I would never let go until he took me back. He hit me again, and again. A chant began in my head that matched the blows of the Indian's fist—*let me go, let me go, let me go.* Then everything went black.

I woke up with a bad taste in my mouth, my head resting on a pillow made of leather.

I forced my eyes open and bright sunlight stabbed my eyes. The smell of horse was strong. I tried to move my head but something held my cheek and wouldn't let go. Then I remembered.

I yanked my face off of the Indian's chest, tearing away the dried blood that had secured my head to my captor's body. The Indian winced as fresh blood leaked out of the wound I'd given him. I was glad. I hoped he'd never heal.

The Indian moved his hand up toward my head. I pulled away but couldn't go far. He murmured something before taking up a section of my hair, and fingering the gleaming strands with great tenderness.

I couldn't help myself. I started to cry. I wanted to be ugly so he would never have taken me in the first place. I knew now that fighting would do me no good. I had a powerful headache to prove it, but I vowed to find a way to escape soon.

When we came within sight of an Indian settlement, I stared at the animal skins stretched over pole skeletons that stood spread-legged along the edge of a stream. The Indians who moved among the crude shelters turned and stared at me before heading toward us with smiles of welcome on their faces and excited chatter flying between them. My captor stopped his horse and waited until another brave jumped from his mount and stood on the ground beside us. Then he slid me down to the arms of this new Indian.

As soon as my feet touched the ground, I renewed my fight for freedom. I would have used my teeth again, but he twisted me around so that I faced out, and clamped me against him. I screamed, and the Indians who were gathering stared at me. I struggled until the Indian who held me lifted me off the ground. I swung my feet back and kicked him in the shins. He grunted and stepped back, dragging me with him.

A sharp command cut through my pounding headache. My

feet touched the ground and I stared up into the face of an Indian with a white smear of paint cutting his face in two. A slash of vermilion scarred his forehead. The effect was startling, as was the raw wound on the man's chest. Trails of dried blood streaked his torso and were lost in the deerskin wrapped around his hips.

I pulled my eyes up from the trail of blood and stared into my captor's face. I hoped he would kill me quickly.

He spoke, but I didn't understand anything he said. His tender voice took me completely by surprise. I stared into his eyes and saw a softness in their depths that didn't fit the savage.

My captor called something over his shoulder. An Indian woman carried a wooden bowl over to him. My captor reached his hand into the bowl. I tensed. He drew out a striped cloth that was heavy with water. He moved it toward my face, and I twisted away from him as far as I could, not wanting to be suffocated.

Instead of pressing the cloth against my mouth and nose, my captor touched it to my cheek. With quick, sure strokes he cleaned away the dried blood.

When he finished, he took me by the arm and the other Indian let go. I pulled away, but I couldn't get free. He anchored me to his side with one arm and guided me through the Indians who gaped at me in open-mouthed amazement. I couldn't tell if they admired my red hair or thought I was a devil woman.

When my captor pushed me inside a tepee, I lost my balance and fell onto a fur robe ingrained with the sharp odors of smoke and sour sweat. I rolled onto my back. My captor gazed down at me with a queer light in his eyes. My stomach churned, and I curled into a ball, tugging my nightdress down as far as it would go.

My captor laughed again and left the tepee. I was momentarily relieved, even though I knew I hadn't seen the last of him.

My limbs felt as weak and heavy as wet laundry. I decided to rest a moment before making my plans to escape.

When I awoke, I was alone. This was my chance. I stood up and took a careful step toward the tepee opening.

Suddenly, my captor stepped into the entrance. Even without

his face paint, I recognized him. I stumbled and fell back again, angry at myself for my inability to appear strong before this savage. I noticed that the trail of blood had been washed away, leaving only the distinct print of my teeth on his chest.

I sat up and yanked my nightdress down over my calves and feet. My captor lowered himself to the ground, never taking his eyes off me. The sight of the wide prairie beyond him tormented me.

The Indian put his hand out toward me, and I scuttled backward, my eyes wide. I knew I didn't have the strength to stop him, but I would do anything I could to cause him pain if he tried anything.

"Deche," the Indian said in a voice that was surprisingly kind.

I shook my head. "No." I didn't know what he'd said, but I wasn't agreeing to anything.

My captor leaned forward and lifted his hand toward me.

"No!" I said, clutching at my nightdress.

The Indian dropped his arm, his eyes alight with interest. He spoke again, longer this time, gesturing out of the tepee before touching himself on the chest. Then he held his hand toward me again.

I shook my head, and felt my fiery hair dance around my shoulders. I wished that I had some hair pins.

"Bambipe ainga," the Indian said, his eyes fastened on my hair. His mouth turned up in a grin. I was horrified to be reminded that my most vehement protests only served to amuse the savage. Yet I still had my teeth, and I curled my lips back to remind him of that fact.

Suddenly, my captor tossed an object that he held in his open hand toward me. I dodged some type of black bread that sailed past me, and my captor grabbed the hem of my nightdress. I screamed in protest and kicked out at him. He grabbed my feet and held them firm. I shrieked. He put one of his palms out toward my mouth, speaking rapidly to me in his own tongue, his voice low and soothing.

This was a nightmare, but I stopped screaming and forced my mouth closed for fear that he would actually put his hand over my mouth if I didn't.

He stared down at my feet—dead white against his dark skin. His touch was gentle as he slid his brown hands around my ankles. I stiffened, my body protesting any contact with this savage. He spoke again, his voice deep and soft. "Andahtese." His eyes traveled up from my feet, taking in the line of my legs, lingering on my torso before settling on my face.

He obviously did not see me as a devil. I kept my eyes pinned on him, watching for any sudden moves.

Suddenly he pulled back and let go of me. I yanked my feet away and tucked them inside my nightdress.

My captor brought out a square of buckskin and held it out toward me. The buckskin was tanned to a dull white and had several red beads threaded onto two leather strings dangling from the center. I wondered what it was for. The Indian thrust the talisman toward me.

Something stirred in the camp beyond the tepee, and the Indian turned his head. I strained to look beyond him, but I couldn't see anything except a few Indians running past the opening.

My captor turned back to me. He spoke again, his voice raised with urgency. "Bahambia," he said. He thrust the ornament toward me, his arm stretched out. It was obvious that he wanted me to take it.

I stared at the ornament with swaying red beads. If I took it, would he leave? If so, might I make my escape now? I lifted my hand toward the offering.

"Livvy!" The unexpected bellow of Josiah's voice cut through the wall of the tepee.

A flood of joy pushed me up onto my feet. "Josiah!" I screamed. "I'm in here!"

My captor leapt up and stepped outside the tepee. I followed him. The Indian barred my way and again held the buckskin talisman toward me.

I stood looking up at him. What should I do? If I took the talisman would he let me go to Josiah? I bit my lip and put my hand out toward the red beads.

"Don't touch that!" Josiah's command split the air.

I dropped my hand to my side, and the Indian spun around to face the dozen white men from the wagon train, who sat on their horses with rifles in their hands. My heart swelled with joy when I saw Josiah in the lead.

I glanced around the camp, gauging my chances of making a run for it. Several Indian men armed with bows, spears, and rifles watched the white visitors.

My captor accosted the newcomers with a rapid stream of Indian words. Josiah leaned forward in the saddle, his eyes fastened on me, though his words were directed at the men in the posse. "He says he stole her fair and square," Josiah translated.

I felt like a jackrabbit was fighting to get out of my belly. The Indians couldn't possibly keep me here now.

"Will he trade?" Zebedee Carson asked.

"Indians will always trade," Josiah answered. He tore his eyes away from me and slid off his horse. He faced my captor and spoke rapidly in the Indian tongue. My hope soared. Josiah knew how to talk to these Indians. I studied Josiah, my heart swelling with a curious mixture of pride and longing. Josiah stood tall and unafraid. His features etched themselves deep into my heart as I watched him bargain for my life. I was so close to freedom that I yearned to run to Josiah, wrap my arms around him, and never let go. Yet my captor was between us, and I feared that I might make things worse if I gave in to my wild impulses.

Josiah drew out a pocket watch and held it toward my captor. The Indian took the watch and held it to his ear. His eyes grew wide with wonder. Then my captor looked over at me where the sunlight glinted off my fiery hair. He shook his head and pushed the watch back into Josiah's hand.

Josiah pulled away, refusing to take the watch, and spoke in the Indian language again. My captor kept his eyes on me. Several of the Indians who were gathered around murmured among themselves. My captor looked at the white men who sat on horses with rifles across their laps. Then he spoke.

"He says it will take much to exchange for this woman," Josiah translated.

"We will trade," Zebedee Carson said without pause.

My eyes filled with tears as my rescuers opened up their saddlebags and handed out knives, watches, tobacco, and other trinkets. Finally, Josiah pulled out a silver box decorated with scroll work.

"No," I whispered. My hand pressed against my chest. Josiah opened the lid and the Indians gasped when the music spilled out over the camp. My captor reached for the box. Josiah let him take it.

The Indian closed the lid, and opened it again, a smile of delight spreading across his dark face when the music started up again. He turned away from Josiah.

Josiah held his hand toward me. I ran to him, and he boosted me up onto the back of his horse. Then he pulled himself into the saddle and turned away from the camp.

I flung my arms around Josiah's waist and hung on shamelessly. I determined not to let go until the Indians were out of sight.

Just before Josiah turned his horse, my green eyes caught sight of my captor's face. His dark eyes bored into mine as Josiah kicked his horse into a trot and we left the Indian camp behind.

The wagons stood in the same place they'd been that morning. Josiah had to pry me loose before he could get down from his horse. He turned and caught me around the waist and lifted me down, his hands warm through the fabric of my nightdress.

Emily Carson grabbed me up in a hug, bulbous tears rolling down her face. "Oh, Livvy, I was so scared for you."

As soon as Emily turned me loose, a pack of Carson boys crowded around me, tugging on my skirt and asking questions. "Where did you go?" "You scream loud!" "I got an owie!" "You made Mama cry." "Are you an Indian now?"

Zebedee Carson waded in. "Now, boys, quit pesterin' Livvy. Go get your Mama some firewood."

Josiah took my arm and led me away from the Carson wagon. "You certainly livened things up around here for a bit, but things will soon get back to normal."

I looked up into Josiah's face and felt my heart twist with disappointment. I never wanted things to be the same again.

"Are you all right?" Josiah asked.

I lowered my head and nodded, fighting tears.

Josiah's hand wrapped around one of mine. When he spoke, his voice came out low, "I couldn't have gone on without you."

I lifted my head and looked into Josiah's eyes, which were dark and soft as night.

"Thank you for rescuing me." My heart caught in my throat. "I'm real sorry about your music box."

"Don't be," Josiah said. "I'd give anything for you."

My heart skipped a beat, and I wiped my eyes. "Anything?"

Josiah's voice didn't even waver when he said, "I'd die for you, Olivia."

Tears burned my eyes, blurring Josiah's features. "Well, if you'd died rescuing me, it wouldn't have done me much good."

"It came awfully close."

"What?"

"We were nearly too late."

"Why?"

"The marriage token," Josiah said.

I was taken completely aback. I didn't remember any marriage token.

"That scrap of skin with the beads was an offer of marriage. If you had taken it, you would have been married to the man who offered it to you. We would have had to battle to the death if we were to take you back with us."

"But you were outnumbered." A shiver of dread ran down my spine.

"I'd have fought for you." Josiah's eyes burned the truth of his words into me. He pulled me in against him and wrapped me in his arms. I leaned my head against his chest and felt his heart beat strong and hard beneath my ear. I knew I belonged there.

"Thank goodness you warned me in time," I said. I tipped my head up at him and asked, "How did you know what it was? And how in the world did you learn their language?"

Josiah's eyes wavered for just an instant, before he straightened and said, "My father was Indian."

My stomach swooped the same way it had when I'd been lifted up onto the Indian's horse. "Your father?" I asked, not wanting to believe it. "He stole a white woman?"

"He didn't steal her," Josiah said, his eyes flashing indignation. "My mother went willingly."

I stared into Josiah's hard, black eyes that were alive with passion. Under my gaze, his eyes softened. "It wasn't like what happened to you," Josiah said. "Mama loved my ah-pey—my father."

Josiah took my hands. I looked down at my white hands buried in his brown ones. They looked good together.

"I believe that a woman should have some say in who she spends her life with," Josiah said.

"I'm glad."

"What would you say to spending your life with me?"

I grinned and pulled one hand free, lifting it to Josiah's head. I slid my fingers through his black hair. "I'd say someone's got to watch over the guard."

Josiah grinned and gave in to the pressure of my hand on the back of his neck. Our lips met.

When Josiah pulled away, he slid one finger down my cheek. Then his eyebrows locked together in mock severity. "Here, now. You'd better change."

I had the decency to blush when I realized that I was still clad only in my nightdress. But after what I'd been through today, it seemed a small matter.

"Why?" I asked. "It's going on evening. I'd just have to change again before I go to bed." I looked up at the clear sky—the pinks of sunset beginning to dust the western horizon. "Anyway, I don't want to miss the sunset. It looks like it's going to be a good night for wishing on a star."

This is a compilation of various experiences I've read about from the 1800s in which Indians captured white women and children with the intent of assimilating them into their tribes. Sometimes ransoms were arranged, but sometimes the captives couldn't be found, and the missing white people were left to their new lives. In some instances when the whites were found at a later time, they were happy in their new lives in the Indian camp and chose to stay with the tribe.

Andahtese: another person
Bambipe: hair
Ainga: red
Deche: quiet
Bahambia: wife
Ah-pey: Father

A Life for a Life

Will Probert dashed through my office door, his cheeks as red and shiny as a newly washed apple and his breath coming as hard and heavy as an apple thief running from the orchard owner. "Bishop!" he said, "Black Hawk's kin just got a beating!"

I jumped out of my chair. "Where? Is he hurt bad?"

Will shrugged. "Who knows? He got knocked around some, beaten down. Then he broke free and made it to his horse. He lit out of here on his own power, but he was bleeding pretty bad."

I stared at Will. "What was the provocation?"

"I wasn't there for the first of it," he said. "I just came at the end." Then he raised a warning finger and shook it at me. "But it's not the end, Henry."

My stomach dropped at his warning. I didn't want to hear about any more trouble, even though trouble was all that we seemed to be having lately when it came to Indian matters. This was war.

In nearly every church meeting I'd conducted since before the war began, I'd spoken of our need to show the Indians mercy—to set the example for kindness. What I didn't speak of was Chief Black Hawk's personal promise to me.

I had made the acquaintance of the chief when I'd been called as bishop three years earlier, and we had struck up a friendship. I found him a fascinating study; he was a mix of old traditions and new knowledge, since he had attended a white man's school as a child. I respected the aging Indian, and didn't wish any harm or trouble to come upon him or his people.

Only a few months earlier, the chief had met me on the road. We greeted each other warmly, and then he stopped speaking and fixed me with his eyes—black and solemn. I, too, fell silent, a sudden uneasiness creeping over me.

"You needn't worry," Black Hawk said at last, his deep voice rumbling. "I promise no harm will come to you and your family."

"Well, uh, thank you," I stammered, not sure why the chief figured he needed to make such a promise. We had always gotten along. We shared our food and clothes with the Indians and they shared their knowledge of survival in this wilderness with us.

It was only after my impromptu meeting with Black Hawk that trouble started in earnest between our two cultures. A few Indians tried to help themselves to some cattle that were grazing in the fields, and the owners tried to stop them. Arrows and bullets flew, and several whites were killed. Then word came that several Indians had been killed in another skirmish, then more white men, then both. The news from other settlements was that war was escalating.

"You know it's an eye for an eye to an Indian's way of thinkin,'" Will said, bringing my mind back to the present problem.

I knew.

"When I was staying over by Scipio, an Indian by the name of Panacara got killed," Will said. "It was a terrible mistake. Panacara was a friend to us. He came vistin' at the fort, and turned in his gun just like he was supposed to. But then one of them whites with a chip on his shoulder follered him real sneaky like and shot him."

Will scratched his chin. "It was a terrible loss, just terrible. And if that wasn't bad enough, Panacara's close friend Nun-ka-tots started follerin' me around. I thought at first that maybe he was just lonesome, but he proved otherwise.

"Came a day I was driving a wagon load of wheat past Mud Lake. When I happened to glance down into the water, I caught sight of a mighty strange reflection. I stared at it, ponderin,' before I realized I was lookin' at a rifle barrel stickin' up in the air. I wondered why I couldn't see it from the road 'til I realized that whoever was lyin' in ambush for me was crouched behind a mound of earth up ahead.

"I drew my wagon up short and pulled out my gun. Before I could get into firing position, I heard scrabblin', and then Nun-ka-tots lit out of there fast as he could go.

"After that, he quit follerin' me around. Then it was a long time before he spoke to me. First thing he sez is, 'You tobuck?'" Will tipped his head toward me. "That means 'angry,' in case you didn't know."

"What did you say?" I asked.

Will raised his eyebrows. "I told him I wasn't tobuck, but why'd he try to kill me anyway? That Indian just looked at me and sez that they avenge their dead by killing one of the enemy—doesn't matter who, it's nothing personal, but they've got to kill one of their enemy in order for their tribesmen's spirit to rest."

I felt a chill roll down my spine. "But you said the Indian boy, Black Hawk's kin, got away."

"He was hurt bad, though. Can't tell if he'll make it. You know, some people die from injuries long after the fact."

I knew. With the way things had turned between our people, and Chief Black Hawk's own kin being so brutally treated in our town, how could I hope to hang on to the promise that he'd made to me? And why did I think I deserved special consideration over anyone else in town? Surely the war made everything that had been said earlier null and void.

The next Sunday, we waited and waited for my son William and his wife, Martha, to come over for supper. They came every Sunday for supper. As it grew later and later, I paced the floor until, finally, I could wait no longer. I got on my horse and rode for my son's place. I was too late. I found Martha weeping and William dead—killed by an Indian arrow.

Black Hawk had lied to me. Even though I'd tried to convince myself that his promise couldn't possibly matter anymore, I found myself furious that he hadn't kept his word. His promise was worthless.

I couldn't leave Martha there alone with her grief, so I took her home with me. Because of her, I held back my tears.

When my wife caught sight of our daughter-in-law, she began to cry before she even heard the news. She had already suspected the worst, and Martha's red, tear-splotched face confirmed it. The women fell together, sobbing, and I sank into a chair with my head in my hands.

I didn't feel like I would ever smile again. What a senseless waste of a young man's life. I prayed earnestly, searching for any shred of peace to soothe my aching heart. But the gap of sorrow was just too big to fill with prayer—I wanted revenge.

I knew this was wrong, so I shut myself in my room and begged for forgiveness. A shadow of comfort crept into a corner of my heart, but it vanished when I opened my eyes and stepped out of the seclusion of my room. I tried in my office with the same result. I prayed several times a day, but the core of anger and hurt remained.

If only William had been taken by illness. Then I would know that his death was the Lord's will. His murder was too arbitrary. He was in the wrong place at the wrong time. His life had been stolen from him, from Martha, and from me. It was all so pointless and cruel; I couldn't seem to wrap my heart around it and soften the sorrow.

It was a long and heavy-hearted week later that found me walking toward home with my hands clasped behind my back and my head bowed. A shadow fell across my path, but I didn't look up right away. I simply couldn't take even one more expression of sympathy from someone who still had their son and had no idea what I was feeling with the loss of mine.

At last, I raised my eyes to see Chief Black Hawk standing before me. His back straight, he fixed his dark eyes on my face. My eyes slid to his hand, which wrapped around the handle of a large knife.

A sudden, fierce anger shot through me. Had the chief come to pick off another of the Kearns family? My fists curled, my jaw clenched, and I stared up into his face, unblinking, to prove that I wasn't afraid.

Chief Black Hawk stared back at me with eyes as deep and

black as an open grave at midnight. He regarded me for a solemn moment before lowering his gaze to the ground. A surge of triumph crowded in with the anger in my heart. I had cowed the mighty chief.

"My grandson died," he murmured.

A strange sense of perverse jubilation gripped me. I would not say I was sorry.

"His brother sought vengeance and killed your son." There was no triumph in Black Hawk's voice, only sorrow. I gritted my teeth at the sudden wave of grief that threatened to overtake me at this blunt reminder of my son's death.

Black Hawk gripped the edges of his shirt and ripped them apart, baring his bronze chest. "I am ready to die in exchange for the life of your son." Black Hawk threw his knife at my feet. He dropped his hands and pulled his shoulders back, making his bare chest an easy target.

His words hit me like a mad bull. I stepped back, dizzy at the prospect of striking Black Hawk dead. My stomach turned over, sickened by the thought of stabbing a knife into his old, brown flesh.

At last, the anger fled completely from my heart, and I put my hand up toward Black Hawk. "I do not wish to kill you," I said, and I meant every word. "I do not wish to kill any of your people." I stopped and swallowed the lump in my throat that threatened to break my words into sobs. "I only want us to stop fighting."

Black Hawk relaxed his shoulders, and his eyes found mine again. "We are still friends?" he asked, his eyebrows rising.

I nodded. "Friends."

Black Hawk put his hand out and clasped mine, his grateful smile big enough to wrap around my heart. "Friends."

Before the Black Hawk War began in 1865, Chief Black Hawk struck up a friendship with Bishop Hamilton Henry Kearns of Gunnison, Utah. The Indian chief promised that Kearns and his family would always be safe

Then one day in 1865, Black Hawk's grandson rode into town and was beaten and driven away. A little while later, perhaps in retaliation, the Bishop's son, William, was killed by an Indian arrow. When Black Hawk heard of the incident, he sought out Bishop Kearns, bared his chest, and declared himself ready to die for the loss of Kearns's son. Instead of killing Black Hawk, Kearns said that he just wanted the fighting to stop.

Before his death, Chief Black Hawk visited all the towns that had received the brunt of warfare during the Black Hawk War and apologized for fighting with them.

William Probert wrote a letter in 1912 in which he described an event that happened to him on the road from Deseret to Scipio in the 1860s after a peaceable Indian named Panacara was murdered by a white man named Ivie.

According to Indian custom, it was a life for a life, and it didn't matter who died in place of the Indian who had been killed. Panacara's friend Nun-ka-tots stalked Probert and then hid along the trail in ambush. Probert saw the reflection of a rifle in Mud Lake and then saw the Indian's reflection. Nun-ka-tots fled and avoided Probert for seven years. Finally, the Indian asked the white man if he was angry with him. When Probert said no, they became friends.

Sources: *Saga of the Sanpitch* 27 (1995): 5; 3 (1971): 27.

A Dying Curse

"Millicent!" I called. I wiped a drip of sweat off of my forehead, muttering under my breath. Millie couldn't be very far away. Why wasn't she answering?

"Millicent!" I called again. I rounded a bush and caught sight of my little sister standing stock still. That certainly wasn't in her nature.

"Millie?" I said, my voice ringing with impatience. She still didn't move. What was the matter with her? Even when she slept, she moved about on her mattress with such energy that it was not unheard of for her to end up on the floor by morning. Now she stared at something I couldn't see, her hands frozen around the waist of her little cloth doll.

I moved toward her and finally saw what she was looking at. An Indian was only a quarter mile away from my little sister, moving steadily closer. He was flanked by two half-grown Indian boys.

Without even pausing, the trio of Indians marched right past the boundary rock that marked the edge of town. I was aghast. The Indians had promised that they would never venture beyond the boundary rock and into the city limits.

I dashed toward my sister. She didn't even look at me. "Millie!" I called.

"Look, Robert," she said, pointing her little finger toward the dark-skinned visitors. "Indians."

I scooped my sister up into my arms, and then turned and ran. It felt like miles before we reached home and burst in through the door. "Indians," I exclaimed.

My mother clenched her hand over her heart. "Where?"

"Inside the boundary rock."

"Go get help," Mama said. She took Millicent from me. "Be quick."

I dashed out the back door and ran toward the center of town. I didn't find my father, but I called out to every man I saw. "Indians! Indians in town!" Within minutes, there were a dozen men running for horses and weapons.

"Lead the way," Clive Austin called out to me.

When we reached the boundary stone, the Indians were no longer there. I wondered if the men would think I was just crying "wolf." I really started to worry about my reputation until someone shouted, "Over there!"

I looked to where the man pointed at the northeast hills and spotted the three Indians on the run. With a sigh of relief, I turned toward home.

A voice rose from the assembly. "Let's get 'em."

Another voice agreed. "Yeah, let's show 'em they can't get away with that!"

A couple of new men came riding up on horses. "Where are those Injuns?" one asked.

"There!"

The horsemen took off after the fleeing Indians. Even though there was no hope of matching their pace, I joined several of the other men who took to their heels and chased after the horsemen.

By the time I caught up to where the horses had stopped, the Indian man and one of the boys were on the ground. The boy, who looked to be about the same age as me, was covered with blood and lying perfectly still, his dark eyes staring up unblinking at the hot, blue sky.

The horsemen were off their horses now, standing over the Indian who clutched at a bloody wound on his chest and grimaced with crooked teeth showing white against the dark skin of his face.

The Indian's eyes turned toward the still youth lying a few yards away. "Ash-tay mik-takken," he muttered, his eyes wet with tears.

"The other one got away," Clive Austin snapped. "But not for long."

"You," the Indian said, his face hard. "We come for pannah," he gasped. "No fight."

"What's pannah?" I asked the guy standing next to me.

"Bread. Those Indians are always after our bread."

"My sons," the Indian clenched his teeth. His dark eyes flicked to the corpse of his son, and then they blazed as he looked at the white men standing above him. "We only come for bread. My sons had no weapons. We meant no harm."

"Easy for you to say now." One of the men said. Then he turned away. "Why are we standing here? I've got work to do."

"I curse you for this cruelty," the Indian said.

An eerie silence fell over the group. Even the man who was in such a hurry to get away stopped and looked back at the Indian as if he couldn't help himself. The Indian's breath came out raspy and weak, but the determination behind his soft words gave them power.

"This ground that soaks up the lifeblood of my innocent son will hold the power of life and not let it free." The Indian gasped and then grimaced. His dark eyes swept the group. "Anyone who inhabits this ground shall have no posterity."

A silence followed his pronouncement. The old Indian let out a moan that chilled my bones. His hand slid off his bloody chest and flopped to the ground, his red fingers curling up toward the sky like the claw of a dead crow that I had found out in the desert one day.

My heart squeezed with pity for the dead Indian, concern for his sons still etched on his face. Even though I feared them, this Indian had only been trying to feed his boys. There was something about him that reminded me of my own father.

Without waiting to see what anyone else was going to do, I turned away from the place of death and headed for home. I needed to find my father.

Arlea Howell told me this story and showed me the boundary stone. Her aunt and uncle owned a house on the very property in Spring City, Utah, where the Indian had died. Although her aunt and uncle had four children when they moved in, they had no more children afterward. In addition, none of their four children had any offspring, a fact that matches the curse pronounced by the dying Indian.

In the mid-1900s, the skeleton of an adolescent was found in the hills east of Spring City. Tests showed that the skeleton was male and was dated between 100 and 150 years old. Arlea speculates that it was the skeleton of the Indian boy who escaped into the mountains but didn't escape death after all.

Ash-tay-mik-taken: have peace, my son
Pannah: bread

Massacre

I lay in my elk skin bed, listening to Ah-peh's worried voice. "But Tin-Dup had a dream," Ah-peh said to Pee-Kage, my mother. "In it, the pony soldiers came into camp and killed all his people."

I shivered in my bed. I'd never seen a pony soldier, but I'd heard about them. They rode horses and carried long sticks called "rifles" that killed people from great distances. I hoped I would never see one in my whole life.

"But what can we do?" Pee-Kage asked. "It is the middle of winter camp. We have nowhere else to go."

"We don't know when it will come to pass, but we have been forewarned. We will watch and wait. I have checked my arrows, as have the other men in camp."

I let my breath out in relief. Ah-peh and the other warriors would keep us safe from the palefaced pony soldiers. Still, not every family had a father, and the warriors of our village had wives, children, and parents. There were more people to take care of than our warriors could defend.

"Ah-peh?" I said.

"Oh, Wy-Ve-Dah, have you been listening when you should be sleeping?" Ah-peh's voice was full of gentle reproach.

"I wasn't asleep," I said, wishing I had been. The even breathing of my older sister, Luc-Ce, beside me made me envious that she was ignorant of Tin-Dup's dream. She would sleep well all night long.

"Well, let me tell you a story about Toowats the eagle, and see if I can help you fly away to the land of good dreams." I settled down into my bed, comforted by the sound of my father's voice, and soon lost myself in sleep.

The next morning I snuggled down into my elk robe bed and squeezed my eyes shut tight. If I pretended not to be awake, then my mother wouldn't notice my eyes open and make me get up into the cold morning.

But Luc-Ce knew that I was faking. "Get up, lazy," Luc-Ce said, giving me a nudge.

"But the bed is so warm," I murmured.

"You will be warm after you get up and move around." Luc-Ce had no sympathy at all. "You need to help with chores too."

Pee-Kage gave me a nudge. "Come on, Wy-Ve-Dah, or no more stories for you at night. I've made some corn cakes for breakfast. You know you like them."

I tried to decide which I liked better, breakfast or staying in bed. Luc-Ce picked up our baby brother, Tah-Sah-Pun, and touched noses with him. Tah-Sah-Pun squealed with delight, but Luc-Ce's smile faded.

"He's wet!" she complained, holding him out away from her. Tah-Sah-Pun kicked his little legs in the air and squealed.

"There's dry moss in the deerskin bag," Pee-Kage said. "Pack some in the backboard and strap him in for me, will you?"

"You silly boy," Luc-Ce said, laying Tah-Sah-Pun down on a pile of skins so she could take up the backboard. It was easy to be delighted with Tah-Sah-Pun no matter what he did. Not only was he our father's only boy, but he had such a good nature that we couldn't ever stay cross with him.

Luc-Ce looked over at me. "Now, see, Wy-Ve-Dah? It's not one bit too cold for Tah-Sah-Pun. He's a big strong warrior, aren't you, Tah?" Luc-Ce lowered her face down close to Tah-Sah-Pun's and he grinned and grabbed one of her long, black braids.

Just then, our father stuck his head inside our shelter. "Who is going ice fishing with me?" he asked.

"I will!" I answered. I loved spending time with my Ah-peh. He was the kindest man in the whole village, and he hardly ever scolded me as I'd heard other fathers do to their daughters. He said it was because I was such a good girl—I didn't need scolding.

Ah-peh lowered his eyebrows in mock severity. "Have you eaten yet?"

"No, but I will right now."

"Then I will wait outside for you. I've got to make you a spear."

I bounced up and down with delight.

Tah-Sah-Pun was snuggled into his backboard, and Pee-Kage slid him onto her back. There was not a chance that he would get cold outside because he was bundled up so well. Neither would Pee-Kage have to change his moss all day, as it would absorb everything he could possibly do to it, and we would only change the moss that night when he was put to bed.

A frightened shout sounded from outside the tepee. Although I was used to people calling to one another throughout our village, this was different. My mind immediately recalled Ah-peh's somber face the night before, when he'd told Tin-Dup's dream to my mother. Sudden fear gripped me, and I wanted to crawl back into bed.

Pee-Kage moved to the doorway of our shelter to look out, and Tah-Sah-Pun stared at me from his place on her back, his round, black eyes solemn. I smiled at him, even though I didn't feel it inside of me, and he gave me a big grin in return.

"Luc-Ce! Wy-Ve-Dah! Come here!" my mother screamed. Since she almost never yelled at us, the sharpness of her voice made my lip quiver.

I moved with Luc-Ce to our mother's side. I turned to look in the same direction my mother had. The hillside swirled with white mist. Through the mist I saw men riding horses—men dressed all the same and wearing funny little clothes on their heads. Some of the strange riders also carried long sticks. My heart leaped up into my throat and I choked. Pony soldiers!

Pee-Kage grabbed my hand in one of hers, and Luc-Ce's hand with her other. She began to run away from the soldiers riding toward us. I threw one look back over my shoulder and saw Ah-peh running toward the enemy, his bow in his hand and his arrow pouch slung over his shoulder.

Ah-peh would protect us. Comforted by the strength of my father, I faced forward and struggled through the snow. It was awfully deep, and my legs were so much shorter than Pee-Kage's that it was hard to keep up with her. It felt as though she might pull my arm from off of my body. I dragged behind her, trying my best to make my legs move faster. Tah-Sa-Pun watched me from his place on Pee-Kage's back.

Loud sounds as sharp as a dog's bark sounded behind me. The barks came louder and more often, sounding like thunder or the growl of an angry bear.

Pee-Kage stumbled, and I nearly fell. Then I saw Luc-Ce tumble forward into the snow. Pee-Kage let out a loud cry—a frightening sound that made Tah-Sah-Pun scrunch his little face up in worry.

Pee-Kage slowed her steps and glanced back at Luc-Ce. I thought my mother would stop and help my sister up, but she didn't. Instead, she held tighter to my hand and pushed forward.

"Luc-Ce!" I called, my eyes drawn to my sister. She didn't answer, or move. She lay face down in the snow, her head and back stained bright red.

I tore my eyes away from my dead sister and let loose a cry of anguish from my aching heart. Tah-Sah-Pun let out a wail, his little face twisted up in fear and misery. Now we were all crying, and running as best we could through the deep snow—running for our lives.

We struggled along beside the river, with other people from our village who were running too. The barking was getting closer and closer. Several other people fell into the snow—fell and lay still, never to move again. I watched as some of the women leaped into the ice-edged river with baby boards on their backs, and children clutched to their chests. Even though the run through the deep snow had warmed me, I couldn't imagine how cold the river water must be. Although too swift to freeze up completely, the water had to be as cold as ice.

Then, impossibly, in mid-wail, Tah-Sah-Pun fell silent. I tore my eyes from the people who were screaming and struggling against the rushing water and glanced up at my baby brother. A bright red-ribbon of blood ran down his tiny forehead into his eyes which were open but unseeing. Little Tah-Sah-Pun with the bright smile and ready laugh was dead.

"No!" I cried, my heart twisting in pain like a snake caught in a thorn bush.

Pee-Kage stumbled forward a few more steps before her legs buckled and she went down. "Mama!" I shouted, but she lay still. Her body on both sides of the backboard was covered with bleeding wounds.

I knew I could never lift her. Terrified, I tried to run. I struggled to escape through the deep snow on my own, but without my mother to pull me along, I could hardly move.

The vibration of hoofbeats drummed through the ground, and I screamed. Then my heel exploded in a burst of hot, searing pain, and I pitched forward into snow that was stained as red as fire. Then all went dark.

A voice spoke to me in the language of white men. I opened my eyes and flailed my arms. The pony soldiers had killed my brother, my sister, and my mother. "Ah-pey!" I screamed.

A voice said something in soft, soothing tones. I looked up into the face of a lady with wrinkles by her eyes—kindly wrinkles like old Tabio in my village had worn.

I was so cold. I had no more fight in me. This white woman was not a pony soldier, so I stopped swinging my arms and let her and her man take me to their home in Franklin, Idaho. They gave me the name of Margaret Young, and I grew up among them, as the only one of my family to survive.

I am grateful to the palefaces that saved me and gave me a white man's name, but in my heart, I am always Wy-Ve-Dah.

This story was related to me by Keith Burdick, whose great-great-great-great-grandmother Wy-Ve-Dah (Margaret Young) was at the Bia-Ogoi (Bear River) as a little girl on January 29, 1863, when Col. Patrick Connor brought his troops down upon the Shoshone winter camp in what is now Idaho. Some of the Indians attempted to escape by jumping in the river, but they drowned or were shot. Some soldiers dashed babies against the frozen ground and ravaged the wounded Indian women. A group of Mormons from Franklin, Idaho, eventually rescued two wounded Shoshone women and five children. Wy-Ve-Dah was adopted by Brigham Young and given the name of Margaret.

Little Indian Emissary

"Hey, Will, do ya want to eat with us?" Sapinay asked.

"Sure!" I said. "Will eating your mother's cooking make me as tall as you?"

Sapinay grinned. "No way! You eat too much white man's food. You'll never catch up to me."

"I notice that you don't mind eating my Mama's biscuits," I said.

"It would be worth it to be a shorty like you if I could eat them every day," Sapinay said. "Come on."

I trotted beside Sapinay through the gully that led to his family's camp. Truth is, I was tired of our winter diet of salt pork and biscuits, and nothing green had come up in the garden yet, so I was plenty eager to taste something new.

Sapinay ran into the tepee without pausing, but I stopped outside and tried to rub some of the dirt off my hands. It was a habit from home that was hard to break. I admired the fact that Sapinay and his family never bothered with the task of washing their hands before they ate.

Even though I'd been friends with Sapinay for years, I'd never eaten anything his mother had made except some dried venison he gave me while we were out playing. Now I ducked into the tepee right behind Sapinay, and his mother looked up from where she squatted by the fire. She grinned at me, showing several missing teeth.

I'd seen her use a matata, or stone bowl, to grind grain and nuts in. She would crush seeds or whatever was in there with several sharp twists of her wrist, using a smooth rock that just fit the curve of her hand. Sapinay told me that he often found grit in his food from the bits of rock that had worked loose from the grinding bowl. Perhaps his mother had a gap-toothed grin because her teeth had broken on pieces of grit. Maybe eating with Sapinay wasn't such a good idea after all. But if I left now, I might appear to be rude.

I rubbed my hands on my pant legs. Maybe I'd be all right if I just took my time and chewed carefully.

Sapinay's mother reached over and plucked a piece from a mass of black dough that sat in a woven basket on the ground at her side. She slapped the handful of dough onto her bare thigh, turning it and slapping it again and again until she'd flattened it. Then she lifted it off her leg and tossed it onto a flat rock set next to the fire. It hissed, and my stomach squoze itself into a nervous little lump.

"Uh, Sapinay, what is that?" I asked.

Sapinay's eyes widened in anticipation. "Cricket cakes."

"Cricket?" The only crickets I knew of were the big, black bugs with stringy antennae and tiny little heads. They were definitely not something I would ever want to eat.

"Do you know what?" I said. "I'm not really all that hungry."

Sapinay cast a sideways look at me. "Well, then, how about if I follow you home and you can give me your biscuits?"

Sapinay's mother interrupted. "You two are so hard to understand," she said. "You don't speak all Indian."

Sapinay glanced at her. "Will speaks our tongue as well as I do."

She tipped her head from side to side as she spoke. "Sometimes you say words I know, and sometimes you say other words, like Will's words."

Sapinay and I grinned at each other. We hadn't even realized that we'd been mixing Indian words with English. We just used whatever language came to mind to say what we wanted to say.

Even though Mama had been after me for the past couple of years to stop hanging around with Sapinay, I hadn't paid her much mind. I knew that her complaints weren't against Sapinay himself but were based on the fact that Black Hawk had been waging war against the whites. It was hard to figure out who started it, but I'd heard that Black Hawk had been caught taking food from a storehouse and had nocked an arrow at his accusers, only to have a bucket thrown over his head. It was quite an insult to have a bucket thunked over top of you just as you were fixing to shoot someone with an arrow. Mama got more vocal whenever someone was attacked and killed, but I wasn't worried. I didn't even feel like a white boy half the time.

"Mama, it wasn't Sapinay and his bunch that did it," I'd say whenever Mama warned me to stay away.

"Well, the ones that did it used to be friendly too. You just never know when someone's going to turn on you, for reasons you don't even understand."

"Sapinay's like my brother," I said. "Nothing's going to happen to me, and I won't let anything happen to him."

I still believed my own words. My worst danger from Sapinay was death by cricket poisoning.

Still, I wished the fighting would stop. If it didn't, we all might be dead soon.

Then, one day, Sapinay told me that Black Hawk was done fighting. I told him that the whites would want a treaty. I never meant to volunteer to act as go-between, but that's how it turned out.

I was home one day when someone knocked on our door. Mama answered it, and then came to my room. "Will? There's a man here who wants you to go to a meeting with him."

"A meeting?" My heart sank like a rock in a river. I hated meetings. "Do I have to?"

"I really think you should. It sounds important."

Important meetings were the worst. Why couldn't we ever do something fun, like have a game of marbles or stick pulling and talk over business while we played?

"Do I have to wear my Sunday clothes?"

Mama smiled, and the worry lines on her forehead cleared. "No, it's not that kind of meeting. Come on."

I followed her out to the parlor and saw a man dressed in a suit coat and trousers. Although dusty, his shoes didn't show a single scuff mark. I wondered if they were brand new. I hadn't seen brand new shoes in years. I didn't usually bother to wear shoes myself, but I did like to slip on moccasins if ever I felt the need to cover my feet.

"Will Frandsen?" the man asked.

"Yes."

"Come along with me."

I looked up at Mama and she gave me a nod. "It's all right, Will," she said. "Go with the man. I'll make you some sugar cookies for when you get back."

I followed the man outside and saw a fine buggy sitting in the street in front of our house. I noticed that it made our house look poorer by comparison.

I climbed up into the buggy beside the man. I wondered if this was what kings felt like. I wished that Sapinay were with me.

The man got the buggy rolling, and in short order we drew up in front of city hall. I took my time climbing down, wondering if I'd ever get to ride in a buggy as fine as that again.

I followed the man inside. There were several other men sitting in chairs and visiting with one another. They stopped talking as soon as we walked in, and they all turned to look at me. "What?" I demanded. I felt like a bug in a jar.

One man, who wore a beard around his chin without a mustache, stood up and faced the man who'd brought me here. "Is this the boy?" he asked. It didn't sound as though he approved, so I stood up straighter and looked him in the eye.

"This is him."

The bearded man's eyebrows went up and he rubbed his chin. He glanced back at the other men. No one said anything, but all their eyes were still on me.

The man with the beard bent down and asked, "Are you Will?"

"Yes."

"Can you really speak the Indian tongue?"

I didn't like him treating me like a little kid, so I answered in my best Shoshone, "Of course I can. Can't you?"

One man in the back of the room with a scar on his nose burst into laughter. The others looked at him with their eyebrows raised.

"Good answer, boy," the man with the scar said, wiping his eyes.

The man with the beard looked at the man who had spoken. "What did he say?"

The scarred man shrugged. "He said he could speak their language, President Young." Then he winked at me. I grinned back at him.

President Young turned back to me, and now his expression seemed more friendly. "Son, do you know that Chief Black Hawk has agreed to end this war?"

"Yeah, Sapinay told me."

"We need someone to go up into the mountains and tell Black Hawk and the other war chiefs that we are here to sign the treaty. Do you know what a treaty is?"

"Yes," I answered. "I go to school, and I listen too."

By now, several of the men sitting in the room were wearing smiles. The bearded man had his hand up over his mouth. I couldn't see if he was smiling or not, but his eyes were crinkled. Maybe he was stifling a sneeze.

"Would you accept the assignment to get Black Hawk and his war chiefs to come and sign this treaty?"

"Why, yes, I would," I said. "Can I take Sapinay with me?"

The bearded man glanced over his shoulder at the others. No one objected. "Whatever you need to do in order to accomplish your mission," he said.

I narrowed my eyes at him when a sudden thought struck me. "This isn't some sort of trick, is it?"

President Young looked genuinely surprised. "What kind of trick could it be?"

"That you're going to send some army men to follow me. Men with guns."

"No, of course not."

"So it's true," the scarred man said. "He's like an Indian himself. He thinks like one."

"Why don't any of you want to do it?" I asked, my mind alive with suspicion.

"They don't know us like they know you," President Young said. "We don't know where they are, either. We need your knowledge of the Indians to contact them for us. You're our emissary."

I thought it over. "All right. I'll go, as long as Sapinay can come."

"Certainly. We'll wait here."

"No tricks?"

"No tricks. In fact, I'd like to give you a blessing before you leave."

I was genuinely surprised. "What for?"

"So you'll be safe from the Indians."

I snorted. "I'm as safe with them as I am right here."

"It would make me feel better." President Young stared at me with mild eyes.

"All right," I agreed. I sat down and folded my arms. President Young and some of the others put their hands on my head. There were so many of them, it felt as though they might push my neck down into my body. As soon as the amens were said, I stood up and headed for the door. Before leaving I turned and said, "We might not get back right away. It depends on which camp Black Hawk is using right now."

"We'll be here."

Once outside, I headed for the hills. When I found Sapinay, he agreed to go with me.

We tracked Chief Black Hawk down with no trouble at all. He was one person who wasn't bothered by our mix of English and Indian because he understood both. Black Hawk put on his best feathers and rode with us down into the valley, accompanied by his war chiefs. I was rather proud of them.

Someone must have seen us coming, because by the time we

reached the city hall, there was a quite a crowd gathered. Being small for my age, I was lost among the bodies, so I didn't even get to see Chief Black Hawk write his name on the paper that the white men stuck through the window. The other chiefs made their marks.

The war was officially over. A few renegades from both sides occasionally forgot that fact and got a cactus spine stuck in their attitude from time to time, which made them stir up trouble. Still, it was good to have peace for the most part, and good to have Sapinay over for supper at my house every once in a while instead of me having to eat at his place.

In 1872, Willard Laurtiz Frandsen was sent at the tender age of nine by LDS Church President Brigham Young to invite Chief Black Hawk and the other war chiefs down from the mountains to sign the peace treaty and end the war. Will was perfectly comfortable playing with his Indian friends, and he spoke their language like a native. According to Willard's daughter, Talula, the treaty was signed through an open window with the Indians outside and the white men inside.

Source: *Saga of the Sanpitch* 17 (1985): 43.

General Store

I stumbled on the steps that led to the front door of the general store, nearly colliding with an Indian man. He jerked away as if I'd brandished a hot iron in his face while clutching a wad of red calico to his chest.

I staggered and caught my balance in time to save myself the embarrassment of falling against him. My sudden movement jarred my son, who whimpered from his place inside a fabric sling on my back.

"Shush, now, it's all right. Hush, Alan," I said, keeping my eyes on the Indian.

The Indian flinched at the sound of my voice. He made me feel uneasy. If I could believe the gossip I'd heard in the general store last week, I was face to face with a suspected spy.

It was hard to believe because, except his obvious fear of getting too close to me, Bill seemed like any other Indian that lived in the village a few miles out of town. The bright red calico peeking out from his dark fingers looked like it was strangling in his grip. If it had a voice, I imagined it would be screaming.

Suddenly, Bill darted past me and disappeared around the corner of the store.

I sagged in relief and slid Alan off my back. "Hush, hush, hush," I said, turning him toward me. As soon as he caught sight of my face, he grinned, and grabbed for my hair. I smiled back. Alan was one of the best things that ever happened to me, right up there at the top of the list with my husband, Jim.

I carried my baby into the store. The first thing I saw was a huddle of Indian women standing at the side of the counter, their hands clutching their meager purchases and their eyes darting up to where Jilly Tanner leaned across the counter gossiping with Mrs. Constance Despain.

Last week, it was Mr. Despain behind the counter and I'd overheard him talking to Fred Harrison about Indian Bill.

"That Bill's a bad'un," Fred Harrison said. "Every time he comes to town, we get a raid on our livestock."

"Could just be coincidence," Mr. Despain said.

Fred grinned, but there was no humor in his smile. He leaned closer. "I follered 'im," he whispered. "I watched him go out of town a different way than he come in. He went a sneakin' around the back roads, lookin' into ever'body's corrals and pens. Then he hurried on out to the edge of town where his horse was waitin' for him. He was up and gone before a gopher could poke his head out of a hole to see what the noise was all about. The very next day, I tell ya, the very next day we had that raid where widow Sanders lost her buggy horse and the Fields' had most of their cattle disappear."

"He's a good customer, though," Mr. Despain said in Bill's defense. "And you have no proof that he's the culprit."

Fred snorted. "It's him, all right, and even a swaybacked horse is worth a sight more than the price of a plug of tobaccy or a yard of fabric. We're gonna keep a close watch on that one from now on."

Fred twisted his head to look out the window, as if he expected to see Bill standing there listening in. "We can't abide no spies comin' in to tell his tribesmen what to steal from who. We won't stand fer it anymore, no sirree." Fred picked at one of his teeth for a moment and then said, "We hang cattle thieves, ya know."

I swallowed hard, finished my business, and left the store as quickly as I could.

Now the five waiting Indian women glanced over at me from the corners of their eyes, too shy to give me a full-faced appraisal.

Dulcie Johnson fingered some balls of wool that sat on a side counter. I said hello before I gathered up the few things that I'd come into town for. I was in a bit of a hurry, since Jim would be home for dinner at dusk, and I still had a long ride home.

I got into line behind the silent Indian women, and we waited for Jilly to finish up her business. Then Dulcie walked up to the counter right into the space between the Indians and Jilly. "I've found what I wanted," she announced. "How much for three balls of yarn? Oh, and I'd like some tooth powder too."

My eyes widened with astonishment, and I glanced down at Alan. He looked back at me, his blue eyes round with wonder at Dulcie's daring. I looked up. "Excuse me, Dulcie, but these women have been waiting in line since I got here."

Dulcie glanced over at me, then at the Indians, then back at me. "So?"

"So they should go ahead of you."

Dulcie raised her eyebrows. "They're just Indians."

"They're people," I said. "They deserve to be treated with courtesy."

Dulcie turned to stare at Constance and Jilly. "What has gotten into her?" she asked, pointing her thumb back over her shoulder toward me.

Constance twisted her mouth up in a semblance of a smile, but she didn't convince me that she meant it. "I'll just be a minute," she said. Then she moved down the counter and bared her teeth at the Indian women. It was a travesty of a smile, and she would have looked much more attractive without it.

I watched while the Indians paid for their needles and candles. Then I stepped aside to let them pass. The women darted their furtive black-eyed glances at me as they left the store.

I took my turn at the counter. "Honestly, I don't see why you're so concerned about a few Indians," Dulcie said, standing straight with her chin raised high.

"They're people, just like you and me," I said.

Dulcie snorted. "Just like us? No, you're mistaken. Just because they've taken to wearing some of our old clothes doesn't make them like us."

"I heard that Black Hawk's daughter nearly scared little Hans Nelson to death," Jilly chimed in.

I widened my eyes in mock horror. "Oh, is that the time when she was putting her generous gift of moccasins on his feet?"

"She should have known it would scare him if she touched him," Jilly sniffed.

"His parents were standing there the whole time," I said.

"That's not the only thing. Why, I saw some little Indian boys the other day wearing trousers for a change, and I thought, 'oh, thank goodness,' but when they turned around I saw that their mothers had cut the seat out of their pants so that they could do their business wherever and whenever they wanted to." Jilly wrinkled up her nose in disgust.

"Sounds rather practical to me," I said.

"Practical?" Dulcie stared at me as though I'd told her that her hair was a tangled mess of snakes. "Are you daft?"

"I just don't think you should go around judging other people," I said. "If you had lived here first and then the Indians moved in, would you have them expect you to adopt their ways?"

"Never," said Jilly.

"Well, I think they deserve consideration too, even if they act differently than we do. You don't have to like my opinion, but there it is."

"Well, in my opinion, you're carrying your child around like a savage Indian," Dulcie said.

My face reddened. "It's very convenient. It keeps my hands free. You should try it some time."

Dulcie laughed in derision. "Not me. I'm a white woman, through and through."

I tucked my purchases into the baby carrier, turned, and left the store. The door shut behind me, but I could still hear muffled voices inside. It didn't take much imagination to guess who they were gossiping about.

I swung Alan up onto my back and stalked out to where my horse waited for me. It wasn't worth explaining to those women that my parents had some good Indian friends who were loyal enough to die for them. My parents returned the sentiment. I didn't need to explain anything to a bunch of tight-hearted women who couldn't even see the worth of a soul, whether it was covered with dark or light skin.

I climbed on my patient horse and headed out of town, not caring if I returned for a long while.

I was more than halfway home when a mouse darted out in front of me, followed closely by a long, green snake. The mouse jumped up in fright at the unexpected sight of my horse's huge leg heading for him, and the snake drew back and hissed in alarm.

My startled horse reared up on his hind legs, trying to avoid the creatures, and I couldn't stop myself from sliding off his back.

"Oh, no, dear God, please save my baby," I prayed as I felt myself falling backwards.

I hit the ground so hard that it knocked the air out of my lungs.

Alan had no such trouble, and screamed loud enough for both of us. I was grateful that he was still alive, but I couldn't even draw breath to call out his name or give him any soothing words of comfort.

I finally worked enough air into my shocked lungs to keep me from fainting.

"Alan," I called. "Oh, Alan, are you all right?"

I struggled to get up, but a stab of pain shot up my leg and through my hip, making me scream. I couldn't get up. I looked down and saw that my foot was turned at a strange angle.

No. Oh, no. My poor baby, I thought.

I tried to twist my torso so that I could get to my son and comfort him. I could only turn far enough to assure myself that Alan wasn't being crushed by my weight, but the pain was horrendous. I couldn't move enough to get the sling off my back, even though my arms ached to hold my son. He cried so hard that it broke my heart, but I could only talk to him and try to soothe him with my voice.

I don't know how long we lay there. I lost consciousness a time or two, and when I came back from the black depths, my little boy's voice was hoarse and strained. Even so, he kept on crying.

We were both going to die on this road before anyone found us. I was beside myself, wondering if Alan was hurt or bleeding. If only I could hold him in my arms to comfort him before we died, it would make our passing sweeter.

The tears that blurred my eyes were more for Alan's distress than my own. Another bolt of sharp pain shot up my leg, and I felt myself falling away again. Alan's cries became fainter and fainter as I faded into oblivion.

I saw a vision of color—swirling hues that shifted and moved in front of my eyes. They swayed and blended into one another, and then separated into distinct colors before blending again. There was a swishing sound like air over wings, and I wondered if it was the sound of death coming for me.

No. I couldn't leave my son. What would happen to him if he were left all alone in the road, strapped to his dead mother's back?

"No," I screamed, trying to fight off the blackness.

Voices came through the haze, speaking a language I couldn't understand. Were they angel voices?

Then I felt someone tugging Alan off my back. I grabbed the strap of my pack and screamed. These couldn't be angels, because angels would never steal my son.

My eyes opened wide, forcing my awareness up from the haze that shadowed the edges of my mind. I stared up into the face of an Indian woman. There were others behind her, and some behind me, and they were stealing Alan. No! They couldn't have my son.

"Get away!" I screamed, and fought the hands that held me back. Stabs of agonizing pain spurred me on to fight like a wounded wildcat for her kitten. The voices that weren't angels spoke soft, soothing words that maintained kindness in the face of my outburst. It frustrated me that I couldn't understand them.

Suddenly, Alan stopped crying.

I whipped my head around, twisting my body until my leg

screamed in protest and I gasped with the pain, the blood draining from my face. Through the gray haze that crowded in on all sides, I saw an Indian woman cuddling my son against her breast, shushing him. When she caught my eye, she smiled at me.

"What's going on?" My husband's shout filled me with joy, and I was free to fall back into the welcoming darkness. I was safe. Alan was safe. And angels looked strangely like Indians.

I woke up in my own bed while the doctor was wrapping a splint tightly against my leg.

"Where's Alan?" I asked.

The doctor looked over at me, his eyebrows raised. "Your son is fine. He's in the other room."

"I want to see him," I said.

The doctor stepped over to the door and called for Alan to be brought in. Jim was there in an instant, with Alan held against his broad chest. I reached out and took Alan into my arms. The instant I held him, my heart nearly burst with relief, and tears coursed down my cheeks.

Jim had his hand on my head, smoothing my hair over and over, his eyes blinking to fight back tears.

"Is he all right?" I asked.

"Perfectly fine," Jim answered. "Thanks to those Indians."

"Indians?" My brow furrowed in thought as I rested my chin on Alan's head, my arms wrapped securely around my son. "I thought I saw angels."

Jim laughed. "You probably did." He dropped a kiss onto my forehead. "They looked like angels to me when I came searching for you and found you lying on the road."

The next day, the five Indian women from the general store came to visit, bearing flat bread singed nearly black and baskets full of berries and a comb of honey.

"Thank you," I said, my eyes filling with tears of gratitude at their kindness.

They examined my splinted leg with admiring eyes, talking back and forth between themselves. They took turns holding Alan. They made me tea and laid wet cloths on my forehead. I hadn't been delirious—angels did look like Indians.

A few days later, my neighbor Ellie came over with a cake.

"Did you hear about that Indian, Bill?" she asked.

"No."

"He's been to town for the last time," she said. "Harrison and several others escorted him out of the city limits and into the foothills. They came back without him, so we've seen the last of him, for sure."

My heart ached for the frightened Indian whom I'd last seen clutching a wad of red calico as though his life depended on it. In all the time it took my leg to heal, there were no more livestock raids, and we never saw Bill again.

In 1870 a family was moving out of Fort Gunnison. The major hostilities of the Black Hawk War had ceased. When they encountered some Indians in their travels, Black Hawk's daughter scared little Hans when she picked him up, but she only wanted to put a little pair of moccasins on his feet.

At around the same time, a young mother helped some Indian women get their turn at the store, even though it wasn't the popular thing to do. On the way home, her horse was startled and she fell off. She was hurt so badly that she couldn't reach her little son, who was strapped to her back. The Indian women from the store found her and helped her.

Bill was an Indian who came into town fairly regularly. A day or two after each one of his visits, there would be an Indian raid and the townspeople's livestock would be stolen. One day, a few of the townsmen escorted Bill out into the foothills and came back without him. The raids on the animals stopped. Bill was never seen again.

Source: *Saga of the Sanpitch* 3 (1971): 6, 15.

Bed and Breakfast

"Dagnabbit, where's that apple I left here yesterday," I mumbled to myself. I cast a suspicious glance at my two oxen. "Did you root it out, Bawl?" At the sound of his name, the ox turned his big brown eyes toward me. He was clearly puzzled, so I turned to fix my other ox, Bill, with a stern gaze. "Was it you?" Bill snorted and shook a fly off his head, totally unconcerned with my accusation.

Since it was obvious that I wasn't going to get anywhere with this line of questioning, I gave up and went back to work.

By the time the light was gone, I still hadn't finished tilling the ground for my spring planting. Whichever ox had stolen the apple that I'd hidden yesterday sure hadn't made very good use of the extra energy.

I led my oxen into the pen at the edge of the field where I'd left them last night. I didn't like leaving them there because there was always a risk that they'd be taken by Indians. Still, it was five miles back to town, and they'd slow me down. I already had precious few hours to sleep before I had to get up and come back early tomorrow. I wanted to get this field tilled so I could plant it.

"You guys stay here and behave yourselves," I said. I cut some long grass from the side of the road and threw it into the manger. "There's your breakfast. Eat up before I get here tomorrow, or you'll be mighty hungry while pullin' the plow."

I got on my horse and headed for home.

The next morning I rode up to the pen where my oxen stood staring at me over the fence. "You ready for work?" I asked. I swung off my horse and turned him into the pen. Then I moved toward Bill and Bawl and glanced into the manger. Instead of the scrambled bits of hay that I expected to see after two hungry bovines rummaged through their breakfast, there was an indentation in the center of the manger grass that was about the length and width of a human body.

"What've you two been up to?" I asked, staring at the hay in confusion. Neither one of them confessed.

Another few days of hard work got the field plowed and planted. I didn't spare the time to wonder much about the odd mornings when I found indents in the manger hay. I did wonder what kind of thieving critter was stealing my lunch, though. It only happened on days I worked straight through noon, not stopping to fetch my tin pail from where I'd tucked it inside the manger. I trusted that my horse would leave it be, since he had no talent for taking lids off of tin pails, as far as I knew. On a couple of those evenings, I was so tired that I forgot and left my lunch pail there. When I came back the next morning, it would be right where I'd left it. I'd pick it up, pull off the lid, and stare down into an empty pail. How in the world any critter could get the lid off in the first place baffled me, but to have the ability to stick it back on again was downright spooky. Even Bill and Bawl wouldn't be able to pull off that kind of shenanigan.

On Monday I left the oxen at the field again. Come Tuesday, I got to work early, ready to irrigate my newly planted field. From the road, I spied a dark shape in the manger. I moved close enough to recognize a person lying there—an Indian, Chief Arropeen, to be exact.

Well, well. I wondered what brought him down to these parts. Had he had an argument with his wife and chosen to spend time with my oxen instead? Or maybe his wives had all ganged up against him, since every chief had more than one.

Well, the reason he was sleeping here was his own business, and I wasn't going to bother him none. If Bill and Bawl didn't care, then it was no concern of mine, except maybe for the food that the chief had taken from my lunch pail. On second thought, I counted myself fortunate that he'd at least left me the pail.

I backed off and went around to where Bill and Bawl stared at me over the fence. "I don't need you guys today," I said. "Just let the old chief sleep, okay?"

I was halfway down the first row, coaxing the water along the proper channel, when I saw Chief Arropeen roll out of the manger and give himself a good scratching. He dug around the edges of the hay for a bit before heading for the hills. I wondered if it was the chief who'd found that missing apple after all. I decided that I'd take Bill and Bawl home tonight and leave a little something from my lunch in the manger for the chief.

Once my crop was up, the deer found out that they liked it—a lot. I figured I'd better get me a fence up right away and try to save some crops for harvesting. I gathered a load of fence posts from the mountains and set to work digging holes. Before I even got all the poles set, I could see that I didn't have enough to go all the way around, but by then it was time for first cutting. The deer hadn't managed to eat everything.

When half my harvest was in, I looked up toward the mountain one afternoon and noticed a trail of dark-skinned people wearing skirts walking down the mountain. They all carried long, dark objects crossways in their arms. When they got closer, I could see that the Indian women bore straight, wooden poles—poles that were perfect for fence posts. Without a word, the Indians deposited the poles at the end of the unfinished fence line. Then they turned and walked back up into the mountains.

I stood and watched them go. Although I hadn't recognized any of them, I'd bet my next foal that they were Chief Arropeen's wives and daughters. I thought that enough poles to finish my fence was mighty generous payback for providing the chief a rudimentary bed and a little breakfast.

Peter Mickel Munk homesteaded sixty-two acres west of Arropeen Valley, which was named for old Chief Arropeen. Some nights when he got done working late, he didn't want to bother herding his oxen, Bill and Bawl, the five miles back to town, so he'd fill the manger with hay and leave them there. Some morn-

ings, he'd find an indentation in the hay roughly the size and shape of a body. When he stashed food at the farm, intent on eating it later, it would disappear.

One morning he arrived early and found Chief Arropeen sleeping in the manger. Later, when Ike had a big fence-building project, Arropeen's wives carried fence posts down from the mountain for Ike to use.

Source: *Saga of the Sanpitch* 5 (1973): 7.

ABANDONED

"What is this?" Captain Emmett's icy voice chilled me like a blast from a January storm. I whirled to face the steel-eyed captain, whose mouth was pulled down in a familiar frown. In one hand Captain Emmett held a portion of honeycomb no bigger than his thumb. His other hand rested on the pistol butt at his side.

"It's nothing," I said, my heart sinking even as I spoke. "It's only a scrap of honeycomb."

Captain Emmett did not move his eyes off my face.

"Where did you get it?"

I held the captain's gaze. "I came across it when I was out hunting."

"And you didn't bother to add it to the provisions for the entire company to draw from?"

It wasn't a question. It was an accusation.

"There wasn't much," I said.

"No?" the captain clearly did not believe me.

"No. I gave it to my wife."

"And why is she more important than any other person in this company?"

"Well, she is with child."

"She is not the only one," Captain Emmett roared. "There are many in camp who have excuses to be dealt out extra food, but you choose to ignore them and cater to your own wife. Is that very Christ-like of you?" The captain did not wait for an answer but growled, "You will not get away with this, John Winn. You will be punished."

Captain Emmett strode away, leaving my soul stinging with

pain composed of shame and anger. Of course I would look out for my wife before any other person, but I hadn't meant to hurt anyone else. I knew that others in the company were suffering too, but hadn't I given up one of my oxen as soon as Captain Emmett told me there was a family who needed it more?

We were well beyond the Missouri River now, deep in the wilds of the South Dakota Territory. It had been so long since I had seen the inside of four walls that I almost couldn't remember what it was like to live in a proper house.

The trek had been hard on us all, but it seemed to have had an especially bad effect on Captain Emmett. The further we traveled, the more heavy-handed he became. His demands were stringent, made in a harsh voice that stung my ears like a whip. When he reduced our rations to two measures of corn per day, saying that the provisions in the wagons were reserved for harder times ahead, I could no longer bear to see my wife suffer. When we made camp to let the worn-out animals rest for a couple of days, I took it upon myself to go hunting. Not only did I shoot a grouse, but I had the good fortune to come upon a stash of wild honey. I carried it home in my tightly woven game bag, and took it straight to my own wagon. My satisfaction at seeing Julia's eyes light up as she tasted the rare treat was enough to fill my soul with sufficient sweetness that I didn't need any honey for myself. Julia pressed it upon me, however, and said that she couldn't bear it if my cousin Jim and his wife Nancy didn't have some too.

I contributed the grouse to the community larder, even though I knew that Captain Emmett and his favored friends would be the only ones to taste the fresh meat. But the honey was for my Julia.

Now Moses Emmett, the captain's pimply faced son, strode up to our wagon to fetch me for trial. He tried to act tough but couldn't pull it off. He was just a skinny sapling of a boy, not even full-grown, although he tried to act like he was. I stared him down until he dropped his eyes to the ground and said, "Come with me."

Captain Emmett paced before a group of men seated on the ground. As soon as he saw me, he stopped and pointed a thick finger at me. "This man is a thief."

Upon hearing this brusque accusation, several of the assembled men sat up straighter and turned their gaunt faces from the captain to me and back again.

Captain Emmett continued, "He admitted to me that he gave his wife food that he gathered while supposedly out hunting for the whole company." Captain Emmett held up the piece of honeycomb, and several of the men leaned forward and squinted at it.

"I found this on the ground beside his wagon," Captain Emmett said. "He confessed that this honeycomb was given to his wife, with none to spare for the likes of us."

"I'm sorry," I said. "I just thought that . . ."

"Shut up! You have admitted your guilt and your callousness, and for your cold-hearted efforts to kill us all, you are condemned to die!"

A sudden intake of breath from the onlookers punctuated the sudden burst of fear that shot through me.

Then the reasonable voice of Max Baker spoke up. "Now, wait a minute." Brother Baker stood up from his seat on the ground. "Maybe John did something he oughtn't to have done, but to kill him for it just isn't right."

Several other men murmured and nodded their heads. Captain Emmett turned his fierce gaze on Brother Baker. "He tried to starve us to death. Do you hear me? To death! When a man tries to take another's life, then he shall forfeit his own. It is God's law! Do you have aught to say against God?"

Max Baker sat down again.

"Now, those of you who are scheduled for the next guard watch shall load up your weapons and dispatch this thief before we retire for the night."

No one moved. Several of the men shook their heads, and I heard one of them say, "Murder." It didn't surprise me too much that no one championed my cause. For one thing, there wasn't much fight in a starving man. And while none of them seemed to agree with what Captain Emmett was doing, he pretty well had his thumb on us all. He claimed that he'd been called by the church leaders to head up our company, but in truth he had taken it upon himself to convince us that we were called to settle in the North Dakota Territory. Clearly, it was up to me to defend myself.

"Look," I said, "I didn't mean . . ."

"Shut up," Captain Emmett said, drawing his pistol and aiming it straight at my face.

"Moses!" he called.

The gangly Moses shuffled over to his father's side. The captain pressed the pistol into his son's hand and helped him point it at me. "He must die," Captain Emmett hissed.

I stared at the barrel of the pistol. At this range, it would be hard to miss. The crazed eyes of Captain Emmett pierced me with blazing hatred.

Moses blinked at me several times over the pistol sights, and the gun barrel wavered. My heart hammered so hard that I was certain it was visible to all, making a perfect target.

We stood like that for a lifetime. I held as still as I could, not even daring to draw breath while I faced the men who held my life in their hands.

"Shall I shoot him, Father?" Moses' voice quavered and nearly cracked.

Captain Emmett's eyes narrowed, and he darted a look at his son. His features softened. "Do as you please, son," he said.

Then something snapped inside me. The thought of my Julia as a widow, standing next to my grave while carrying our child, made me so angry at this despot who threatened me with death that I pulled back my shoulders and stood erect. I grabbed the front of my shirt and pulled, popping the buttons off in a spatter of bright orbs sailing through the air and landing with soft plops in the dirt.

"Shoot, you cowardly rats. I dare you to," I bellowed, shifting my gaze from the gun barrel to the captain. There was no compassion in his eyes, but a sudden look of fear flitted across his face.

Moses lowered the gun and handed it to his father.

"This has gone far enough," Max Baker said, rising from the ground. "What John did is no killing offense."

"Brother Baker is right," Jeb Carter said, struggling to his feet. Several other men pushed themselves up from the ground and stared at Captain Emmett.

The captain turned his back on them and holstered his gun. "You will not be shot," he said. "But you will not eat from our stores. You will get your own food." Then he stalked toward his wagon with his son trotting along behind, leaving me standing before my peers.

I turned toward the hungry faces staring at me. "I'm sorry," I said. "I didn't mean to steal from anyone. When I found the honey, all I could think of was Julia and our unborn baby."

Several heads nodded, and Max Baker said, "I would have done the same myself."

I put my hands out toward my fellow travelers. "Besides, there is plenty in the wagons for us to eat. I don't understand why the captain isn't more generous with our rations."

"Perhaps he knows something that we don't," Max Baker said. "We shouldn't question our leader but must follow his advice if we are to survive."

I had my doubts, for what good would it do for us to reach our homesteads in North Dakota if half of us died from hunger?

The next morning, Captain Emmett strode toward our wagon, his cold granite gaze fixed on me.

"Get behind me!" I said, stepping in front of my wife.

"What is it?" Julia asked.

I didn't have time to answer before the captain bellowed, "John Winn, for your crimes against this company, you are to be left behind, to care for yourself and your wife however you see fit."

"No!" I said, thoughts of slow starvation and watching Julia die in agony creating a far worse fear in me than being shot.

"You can't do that!"

"I am the leader of this company, and I do what is best for all. Leaving you behind is best."

"John?" Julia's voice cut through the heavy silence that followed Captain Emmett's pronouncement. My wife's fearful question cut me to the very quick of my soul.

"It's all right," I murmured, even though I didn't believe my own words.

"Now we leave you," the captain said.

"No!" Julia wailed. "You can't do this! My baby!"

"We'll just get our things," I said, moving toward the wagon. I desperately searched my mind for everything I could grab in the precious few minutes I had that would best help us survive.

"No!" the captain bellowed. "You have no things. You are as you are. Make your way as best you can, just like you did before."

I stared the captain in the face. "This is murder," I said.

The captain grinned—an evil twist of his lips that set my hair on edge.

"You will stay behind," the captain said. "Now—move."

I didn't move until the captain drew his gun and shot a bullet into the ground at my feet. Then I leapt back, dragging my wife by the arm.

"No!" Julia screamed. "I need my things!" She jerked her arm out of my grasp and stumbled toward the wagon.

Another shot rang out from Captain Emmett's other pistol. Julia staggered back.

"Julia!" I screamed, and ran to my wife's side, slipping my arm around her waist and holding her close. I couldn't see any blood.

Julia turned to the captain. "You are a beast! A heartless monster! What am I to do when my baby is born? I need the flannels and clothes and blankets I've made with my own hands." Julia lifted her hands toward Captain Emmett in entreaty. "I need my own clothes. How are we to survive with nothing?"

"Now you'll see how the rest of us felt while you enjoyed your sweet treat of wild honey," the captain sneered. "Now you are the ones who will have to do without, so see how you like it."

"No matter my crime, if you truly believe me guilty of anything, my baby is innocent. I need my baby's clothes," Julia said. She pulled herself up and stared the captain in the eye. "I will not leave without them."

"You will not have them," the captain said.

Just then, Nancy appeared from the behind the wagon with two satchels in her hands. She made straight for Julia, not even bothering to glance Captain Emmett's way.

"Here you go, Julia, for you and your baby," Nancy said.

"Oh, thank you, thank you!" Julia cried, reaching for the cases. I put my hand out and grasped one of them, hoping that Nancy might have thought to put a gun and some ammunition in it.

"So, you wish to join them?" Captain Emmett asked, his voice as hard as flint.

"What?" Nancy's eyes darted up, and she stared at the captain.

"Nancy!" Jim called, hurrying over to us. "I was down at the river and heard gunshots. What's the trouble?"

"No trouble," Captain Emmett said. "Sister Wilson has decided that you will stay behind with Brother and Sister Winn while the rest of us move out."

"What?" Jim's eyes went wide with disbelief.

It took some explaining, and more arguing, before Jim and Nancy finally found themselves standing beside us, watching the wagon train pull out. There were many faces pointed our way, watching us recede into the distance, but no one challenged Captain Emmett in his decision. They were too weak and depressed from hunger and fatigue to put up a fight. I didn't believe that anyone besides the captain thought that we deserved this punishment for my indiscretion.

I turned away before the wagon train disappeared. I couldn't bear to see our lifeline go over the rise and disappear from sight.

"Come on," I said, picking up Julia's satchel as well as the one I held. "We'll probably be just as well off on our own as we were with that despot."

Julia sobbed. She didn't believe my words any more than I did.

Nancy hadn't thought to put anything in the satchels besides clothes. She was sorry for it too, but there was nothing to be done about it now.

More than once over the next few days, I suggested that we leave the satchels behind, as they were doing us no good.

"No!" Julia said. "They're for our baby." She threatened to carry them herself if I did not, so I kept carrying them, with Jim to spell me off.

We tried prying roots out of the ground with sticks, but it was a long and tedious process, and we didn't get much. We had no way to cook any of the roots we dug, so we ate them raw. Some of them cramped us up inside, either because they weren't good for us or because our stomachs were so crazed with hunger that they ached when we put food in them.

We didn't have the good fortune to come across any more honey, nor did we find any berry patches with ripe fruit. As we trudged along beside the river, I longed for a simple fishing line. Every fish that jumped out of the water mocked our hunger. Whenever I caught sight of a bird on the wing, my hands itched to hold a loaded gun.

After a few days, I could hardly pick up my feet. Julia was a walking ghost of herself. Nancy and Jim were in bad shape too. The two measures of corn that we'd been allotted in the wagon train seemed generous beyond belief.

I dragged my feet forward with my eyes on the ground, when Jim suddenly cried, "Look!"

I raised my head and saw a cloud of dust in the distance. I made out riders on horses. Squinting my eyes brought lances into focus—their points bristling the air, their ends fluttering with what looked like feathers.

"Indians!" Nancy squeaked.

"No!" Julia said, her voice tight with fear.

"Hide!" Jim said, pulling his wife by the arm toward a screen of brush that was near at hand.

"Wait!" I said. "Perhaps we can ask them for help."

Jim's eyes widened in disbelief. "Ask Indians for help? Are you daft?"

"Look, Jim, we are in a bad way. We need food. At least it's a chance."

"I don't like it."

"Neither do I!" I exploded. "I don't like any of this! I didn't ask to be stranded."

"John," Julia said. "Jim is not our enemy."

"I'm sorry," I said. "But don't you see that they're our only hope? We've got to ask them for help."

"First say a prayer," Julia said.

I stared down at my wife. Her cheekbones jutted out beneath her calm blue eyes.

"Yes, Julia, all right," I said.

We bowed our heads and offered up a prayer from the very center of our hearts and souls. Then I looked at the ladies. "Stay hidden," I said. "Don't come out for anything, unless you hear me or Jim call to you. Do you understand?"

Nancy and Julia nodded from where they crouched side by side, holding on to one another.

Jim and I headed for the band of Indians. It looked like they were passing us by, moving away at an angle, riding their horses faster than we could walk.

"Run!" I said to Jim, now desperate to make contact with these native people who hadn't always proved merciful to whites.

But we were dying anyway. If we had to die, perhaps it would be better to go swiftly at the hands of the Indians than to waste away from hunger.

I pulled my hat off my head and waved it in the air. "Hey!" I called. "Hey!" My legs wobbled beneath me when I tried to run.

Jim called out. "Over here! Wait for us!"

I ran harder than I'd ever run in my life, weaving from side to side as my undernourished body struggled to meet the demands I made of it. I felt light-headed, and for a moment it felt as though I was outrunning myself, my spirit soaring ahead of my emaciated body to turn the heads of the Indians so that they could see us stumbling toward them, our hats raised and our arms reached out in supplication.

The Indians pulled to a stop. Their horses milled about and stamped with impatience.

My heart surged with relief. As we drew closer, the braves on horseback readied their bows and raised their rifles, their wary eyes upon us.

Two braves slid down off their horses and walked toward us, their rifles aimed at our hearts.

"We need help," I called.

"You give guns, give knives," one of the Indians said. Furry strips of animal skin were woven into his braids, and a band of what looked like bear claws circled his neck.

I held both of my hands out. "We don't have any guns or knives," I said.

"We see."

Bear Claw turned to his companion and said something in Indian. Then he held his rifle steady on us while the other Indian came closer and searched us for weapons.

"We were left with nothing," I said as the Indian felt in Jim's pockets. I hoped that my admission was not a mistake. They could easily take advantage of a couple of unarmed whites, but what did it matter what I told them? They were bound to find out our true state of affairs sooner or later.

"Where go from?" Bear Claw asked.

"We were with a wagon train, and they left us behind."

"Sick?" Bear Claw took a step back from us, his eyes narrowing in suspicion. His companion joined him, his rifle raised toward us as well.

"No, no, we're not sick," Jim said. "We're hungry." He opened his mouth and pointed to it.

"Come," Bear Claw said, motioning with his rifle.

He led us over to a middle-aged Indian man, who stood on the ground beside his horse, glaring at us from under dark brows, his arms folded across his chest and his hair bristling with feathers. I was fairly certain that this was the chief.

The chief spoke to Bear Claw in Indian, and Bear Claw said to us, "Who sent you?"

With Bear Claw interpreting, we tried our best to convince the chief that we were left alone by our fellow whites, and had no intent to harm them, but the chief kept a suspicious eye on me.

"Please," I said. "Our wives are starving. We just need some food. Then we'll trouble you no more."

Bear Claw's eyes widened. "Wives?"

"Women," I said, putting my arm out to include Jim. "Our women."

Bear Claw turned and spoke rapidly to the chief. The chief gave a start and glared at Jim and me before he called out an order and three braves appeared at his side.

"You shouldn't have said that," Jim said.

My heart sank as Bear Claw grabbed Jim by the arm. "You stay," he said to me.

"No! Wait!" I cried, but a rifle barrel jabbed into my stomach silenced me.

Bear Claw pulled Jim back the way we had come, with two other braves trailing along behind.

I wanted to rip my own tongue out. How could I have betrayed our wives like that? I couldn't bear the thought of what these savage Indians might do to them. Even though they hadn't hurt us yet, their guns, spears, and arrows had been constantly at the ready, poised to kill us at a single command from their chief.

I risked a look at the chief's face, hoping to find any hope of mercy there. His features were so impassive that they could have been made of wood. My heart quailed within me, and I turned again to watch Jim's stumbling progress.

All too soon, the three Indians were heading back with Jim, Nancy, and Julia. One of the braves even held Julia's arm. My fists tightened at my sides, and I pulled myself up erect.

"Do not harm them," I said.

The chief glanced over at me but didn't say anything.

When Julia was close enough, I reached out to her and she came into my arms. I held her close until I caught the chief watching us. When we broke apart, his gaze traveled down to my wife's distended belly. He said something to Bear Claw.

Bear Claw looked at Julia and pointed at her stomach. "You child?"

Julia cupped a hand protectively around her middle. "Yes."

The chief nodded, and gestured toward a spot where the Indian women had begun setting up camp. I hadn't noticed their activity, since my attention had been on my companions.

We walked over to the wickiups that were rising quickly from the prairie floor. I kept my arm around Julia, and Jim helped Nancy. The sight of our starving wives must have touched the old chief's heart.

We were each taken apart from the others and questioned separately, with Bear Claw acting as an interpreter for the chief. Ultimately, he seemed satisfied that we were all telling the same story.

The chief called out a command, and the braves gathered around him. They spoke among themselves briefly before the young braves broke off and scurried like rabbits, putting on war paint and feathers, shouldering their weapons, and leading their horses to assemble around the chief.

Jim and I both jumped up from where we had collapsed onto the ground. "What are you doing?" I asked Bear Claw.

"Where's everyone going?" Jim asked at the same time.

"We go, kill all who leave you," he said. Then he gave us a nod and started away.

"No! You can't!" I yelled.

Bear Claw looked back over his shoulder, surprise evident on his face.

"They're good people," Jim said. "Only the captain is at fault."

"No good people," Bear Claw said. "Better dead." He strode away from us.

"What are we going to do?" Jim asked.

"Stop them, John," Julia said, pushing herself up from the ground with some difficulty.

"I'll try," I said. I followed Bear Claw with Jim at my heels. By the time we caught up to him, he was talking to the chief.

"Please don't do this," I said. "Those people are our friends."

Bear Claw said something to the chief, who looked at us with disdain. He spoke a single word.

Bear Claw turned back to us. "No. You not right. We kill."

"No, please, you don't understand," I said. "It's not all of them who did this."

"They're good people," Jim added.

"No good leave you," Bear Claw scoffed.

No matter how hard we protested, the Indians were determined to carry through on their plan to massacre the entire wagon train. The chief called out another command, and all of the Indian warriors leapt up onto their horses and turned them in the direction we had come from.

I was at my wit's end. Our friends were already suffering enough under the leadership of the tyrant Captain Emmett. They didn't need any more trouble heaped upon them.

The chief's cold eyes shifted to something behind me, and I turned to see my Julia stumbling toward us. Her eyes, brimming with tears, were fixed on the chief.

In spite of her hollow cheeks and cracked lips, Julia had never looked more beautiful to me. My wife walked up to the chief and sank down onto her knees at his feet. Her face upturned, her hands clasped in front of her, she looked up at the Indian chief and said, "Please, don't kill them. Please, don't kill them." Tears coursed down her cheeks, making silvery trails that slid down her throat and disappeared into the neckline of her dusty dress. Then Julia bowed her head and sobbed.

The chief looked down on Julia's head, his dark eyes inscrutable. I had to blink the tears from my own eyes before I saw the chief raise his eyes to his mounted warriors. He called out a command, and the braves dismounted.

I stared at the warriors as they walked their horses back to the wickiups.

"You stopped the attack!" I cried to the chief. "Thank you! Oh, thank you!"

The grim-faced chief raised his hand, palm toward me, and turned and walked away.

Then Julia collapsed, toppling forward from her knees until she lay on the ground as still as death.

"Julia!" I cried, bending over my wife. Before I could lift her up, I was pushed aside by several Indian women. They carried her into a wickiup and laid her on a bed of buffalo robes.

I tried to follow my wife, but I couldn't get close because of all the Indian women who were seeing to her needs. Jim and Nancy joined me, and we were soon fed a simple meal of jerky, parched corn, and broth. I'd never been so hungry in my life, and the simple food tasted better than anything I'd ever eaten before.

Julia soon fell asleep. We rapidly followed suit, exhausted and finally free from sharp hunger chewing out our insides.

It was early light when I awoke. For a moment, I wondered where I was. The Indian camp was strangely silent. I stuck my head out of the wickiup and looked for our rescuers. They were gone.

I pulled myself outside and looked around. No one was in sight, but on the ground was a buffalo robe folded over itself. I lifted the top fold and stared at what lay inside. A generous supply of jerky, parched corn, a few potatoes, and a couple of cooking pots were nestled in the folds of the robe. My eyes blurred as I stared at this bounty.

Then I heard a horse blow out of its nostrils, and whipped my head around. Jim crawled out of the wickiup, his eyes wide with surprise. Then, as one, we moved around the shelter and found three ponies tethered to a log at the back of our camp. Beside them was an American pack saddle.

I was astounded at the generosity of the Indians who had left three of their precious horses behind for us to make our escape. When I compared the hearts of the savages to the one that beat in Captain Emmett's chest, I knew who the true savage was.

We wasted no time in saddling one of the horses and packing our new belongings onto him. Jim struck the small wickiup, and tied it onto the saddle while I rolled up the buffalo robes we'd been sleeping on. When I lifted the last robe, I was utterly astonished to discover a cap and ball rifle, a generous supply of ammunition, and a hunting knife.

Overcome with gratitude, I fell to my knees and buried my face in my hands.

"John?" Jim called out. "Are you all right?"

I pointed at the ground. "Look what they left for us," I choked out. "They gave us a rifle, Jim. They gave us one of their own rifles."

"Praise be!" Jim called out.

"Jim," I said, wiping my eyes. "I need you to witness my vow. From this day on, I will help and aid the Indian race at every opportunity."

Jim nodded, unable to speak.

We gathered up our precious rifle and ammunition, secured our packhorse, and helped our wives up onto the other two horses. Then, with light hearts and sure steps, Jim and I grabbed the lead ropes and headed toward the morning sunrise.

In 1845, John Winn and his pregnant wife, Julia Anne (or Mary Jane) Akes, joined a wagon company headed by Captain James Emmett. Emmett claimed to have been called by Church authorities to take a band of settlers to North Dakota after the Mormon prophet, Joseph Smith, died. His claims later proved false.

The tyrannical Captain Emmett abandoned the Winns on the trail for the crime of supplementing their meager rations with wild honey. John's cousin Jim Wilson and his wife, Nancy, were left behind too.

A band of Indians, probably Sioux, took them in. Winn's party had to convince the Indians not to massacre the wagon train in order to avenge them. The Indians fed the wanderers and let them sleep in a wickiup.

The next day, the Indians were gone but had left provisions behind. Before they headed back to their families and safety in Nauvoo, John vowed to help and befriend Indians at every opportunity. By the time they arrived back in town, Julia had given birth to a baby boy named Minor.

Captain James Emmett was last seen heading for California in the company of two Indian women.

This story was taken from two separate accounts that differ on a few points, though the events were markedly similar.

Source: David Scott submitted this fascinating story from his family's history.

Two for Two

I wasn't there when the Indian cursed the school. Heck, I wasn't even born yet. Dad was just a boy when it happened, but the event made such an impression on him, and he told it often enough, that I might as well have been right there on the spot.

"Danny-boy, don't blame old Chief Washakorie," Dad would say. "He gave us fair warning."

That may be, but what good's a warning if no one listens?

The trouble really began in 1893, when they started construction of the new Spring City school. I don't know exactly how the old chief caught wind of the building project, but he showed up at the place just as a couple of men were putting their shovels in the ground to hollow out the basement.

"Don't dig here," Washakorie said, his lined face and hard, black eyes as unyielding as a balky mule. His black braids were shot through with the silver of old age, but he was far from feeble as he confronted the white men, his back straight and his arms folded across his chest.

"But, Chief, we've got to. This is where the new school's going," Stanley Hodge said.

"Not here," Washakorie insisted, his voice rolling out in warning like the ominous rumble of boulders crashing down a mountainside. "This is sacred burial ground."

Stan Hodge glanced over at Jack Bawden, who grinned, shook his head, punched his shovel into the ground with his foot, and pried out another plug of dirt.

Stan looked back at the old chief. "Now, now, it'll be fine," he said. "If there really are any of your tribe here, we'll cart 'em on up to Indianola and put 'em to rest beside your other ancestors."

"No!" Washakorie said.

During this exchange, Jack Bawden kept on shoveling, paying no mind to the argument. Washakorie folded his arms in disapproval and watched with hawk eyes as the two men continued digging. Stanley wished mightily that the Indian would just move along, but Washakorie didn't act like he had anything better to do.

Not even a full hour into the digging, Jack Bawden's shovel came up full of dirt mixed with bones—human bones.

Washakorie stalked over to the dig and glared down at the pieces of skeleton. Then he pinned Jack with his fierce, black eyes. Washakorie pulled himself up straight and tall, looking for all the world like an Indian warrior in his prime instead of an aging man. "Now stop," he said.

Stan looked up and wiped his brow. If he were being honest with himself, he was as unnerved by the authority in Washakorie's voice as he was at the sight of the bones. He'd been sure that Washakorie's claim to an ancient Indian burial ground was just an old man rambling.

"Put them back," Washakorie said, jabbing his finger at the scarred earth.

The two diggers looked at each other. Stanley nodded. He was all for filling in the holes, and he couldn't even tell you why. It was like a chill wind blew over the bald spot on top of his head, even though he was wearing his old felt hat. He was shivery clear down to the soles of his boots.

This time it was Jack that turned toward the Indian. "We can't stop. We've got a school to build."

"Not here," Washakorie said, his black eyes staring holes into Jack.

"Look, we'll get these bones out nice and easy, treat 'em with all the respect in the world. Then we'll re-bury them."

Washakorie shook his head once with enough force to kick his braids into a brief and macabre dance around his shoulders. "You desecrate sacred ground."

"We can't hold up the entire construction project for a couple of old skeletons." Jack's impatience was obvious. "We'll just move 'em to the graveyard."

Washakorie's eyes hardened into two points of flint. "No," he said. "Leave them."

Well, that Indian made a real nuisance of himself. Jack went for reinforcements, and Stanley followed, unwilling to stay alone with Washakorie. There was something different about the old Indian—something Stan had never seen before. It was almost like he was someone else, as though the spirits of those dead Indians stood on either side of him with weapons brandished and murder in their eyes.

The two men soon returned, their courage bolstered in the company of several other men. A couple of them took hold of Washakorie's arms, but the Indian pulled free. He turned and strode away, but before he was out of earshot, he turned to face the white men.

"You'll be sorry," he said before he turned and left. He didn't shout, only spoke just loud enough for all of them to hear, but his words paralyzed the group as surely as if he'd smacked them with a shovel. They stared after him, and it was only when he was out of sight that they got back to digging.

The dedication of the new school took place in 1896, the very same year that Utah joined the union of The United States. Dad said it was quite a celebration. There was a band, banners, flags everywhere, and people dressed in their Sunday best, on a weekday, no less. The horses wore polished tack, and normally dusty carriages shone. Some were decorated with garlands, and some with ribbons woven through the wheel spokes.

No one worked in the fields that day. All the households contributed to a community picnic, putting their rolls, deviled eggs, and fried chicken on big tables set up on the new school grounds. It was bigger than the Fourth of July.

Before the new school bell sounded to signal the start of food and games, the mayor stood up at the podium. All the kids groaned. They wanted potato salad and pie, not long-winded speeches.

"We have gathered here today on this most momentous occasion," the mayor began. "How fitting that in this historic year of statehood, we also witness the dedication of our new school." He stretched his hand toward the three-story edifice behind him, and there was a smattering of applause. Some of the kids clapped too, but that was because they hoped that he was done speaking so they could help themselves to the food table.

Before Mayor Christensen could resume his speech, a tall figure with long, black braids shot with silver walked up toward the front of the crowd.

A voice called, "Get back."

Someone else said, "The mayor's talking up there." A general murmur arose, but the Indian ignored it all. He reached the front of the assembly, spun on his heel, and faced the audience. Every eye was on Washakorie.

"I curse this place," he said, his loud voice carrying in the sudden stillness. "You disturbed the spirits of my people. In return, they will occupy this building for a hundred years." A couple of men stood and advanced on Washakorie. He ignored them and swept his gaze around the crowd, pointing a finger at the school. "For the two Indians whose bones you broke with your shovels, two white men's lives are demanded!"

The men grabbed Washakorie, but he broke free.

"I'll go," Washakorie said. He strode off a few paces, and then turned and shouted, "Two for two!"

Then the Indian took off down the road, not running, but moving out in that peculiar gait that takes the Indians for miles and miles without breaking stride.

The men watched him long enough to satisfy themselves that he was really gone. Then one turned to another and shook his head. "Crazy Indian."

The mayor straightened his lapels, cleared his throat, and started up where he left off, much to the dismay of the hungry boys in the crowd. Their hope, that Washakorie's speech would replace what the mayor had to say, was in vain.

By the time I started school in the 1930s, Washakorie was dead and buried, but he left his curse behind. It didn't occur to me until later how unfair it was that we had no part in digging up those bones, but we had to bear the brunt of the curse. Yet, on that first day of school, none of this worried me. I was simply excited to be there.

It's true that I'd heard the stories about the haunted school piano from the older kids. But I knew from personal experience that they lied about things like what's poison oak and what isn't, so I wouldn't admit to believing their spooky stories.

Even though I doubted their word, I was relieved to discover that the piano wasn't in my classroom. Instead, it sat alone in its own room across the hall. Even though the school bell summoned us to line up at the school doors every morning, it was nice old Mrs. Wintch's job to sit at that piano and play a catchy marching tune when it was time for us to come inside, go home for lunch, and come back in for afternoon classes. Whenever I passed the piano room, I'd peek inside and see Mrs. Wintch pounding the keys with gusto. It always surprised me to see such an old lady playing such lively tunes. The cheery melodies that rolled off her fingers made you want to swing your arms and tap your toes.

One day in the fall, the school sat solemnly under a gray sky, leaves outside fading from brilliant red and gold to rusty iron and moldy wheat. It wasn't a very cheery day, to be sure, but Mrs. Wintch's come-inside melody helped lift my mood some.

I remember that my class was busy practicing writing our alphabet letters, because I was concentrating on the intricacies of the capital "B" with my tongue sticking out, and I almost bit it off when the first unexpected piano chord sounded. I pulled my tongue in and lifted my head along with everyone else in the classroom. Our eyes turned in unison toward the door.

Somber, ominous notes floated through the doorway and sent

a shiver down my back. I knew I was supposed to stand, but I didn't. The last thing I wanted to do was line up and march out into that hall. Cold prickles raised up along the back of my neck, but I didn't dare to reach my hand back and rub them down. I didn't dare move at all. I was flooded with a sudden fear that if I so much as blinked, something awful would see me, and some terrible thing would happen to me. What, I didn't know, but I didn't want to find out, either.

"Whatever in the world?" our teacher, Miss Jenkins, said. "Stay where you are, class." I obeyed, frozen to the edge of my chair with my hands gripping the seat. Miss Jenkins disappeared through the doorway.

I was scared for her—I really was. I didn't have any idea why Mrs. Wintch had changed her tune. I hoped that Miss Jenkins would tell her to stop scaring us.

Suddenly, another thought struck me. What if it wasn't Mrs. Wintch playing the piano? What if the principal had hired a new teacher?

The music stopped. Miss Jenkins appeared in the doorway, her hand pressed over her heart like when we said the Pledge of Allegiance. Her face was as white as the chalk on the blackboard ledge.

Alice Kinsey raised her hand. "Who was it?" she asked, not even waiting to get called on.

Miss Jenkins seemed to have difficulty focusing her eyes on Alice. "No one," she said. She moved toward her desk. "It was no one."

Then Miss Jenkins grabbed a book as though it was the last stick of wood in a winter camp, and opened it up. "Let's read a story together, shall we?" she asked, her face smiling but her voice unnaturally high and tense. We put our writing practice papers away and folded our hands on our desks to listen.

This wasn't the last time I heard that death march music, and it wasn't the last time it sent cold prickles squirming down my back.

One of the best things about school were fire drills, especially after I moved to the older grades on the top floors. The fire escape was a curved slide, slanted down from the third-floor windows and turning the corner of the building at the second story level to allow students from that floor to climb out their window and escape the pretend fire. The third floor was best, because you got the longest ride.

At the sound of the school bell, the little kids on the first floor had to line up and march out the door with their teacher. This was a good arrangement, because some of them were too scared to slide down. Even some of the second floor students would scream and cover their faces when told to get on the slide. When this happened, their teachers led them down the stairs. They didn't know what they were missing.

Us lucky students in the high school classrooms on the third floor scrambled for the designated fire escape window as soon as we heard the signal. We'd shift our feet and whisper and nudge each other until the teacher said, "All right, single file, be courteous. Now, go!" Then we'd whoop and holler and scramble out the window onto the metal chute.

Sometimes when we passed other windows, kids would try to cut in and hop on the slide ahead of us. It was quite a scramble, as we could get zipping along pretty good from the top floor. It was great.

We older boys were instructed to wait at the bottom of the slide and catch the younger kids when they came flying down. Some of them weren't coordinated enough to land on their feet but would instead go sailing off the edge with their legs out straight and end up with a rude bump to their behinds.

It was no trouble for us to catch the little kids, especially when the girls from our grade stood around to watch us. I imagined Polly with her eyes pinned on me as I stretched my muscular arms out to catch the children. I hoped she was impressed.

I'll never forget the spring day when the bell rang loud and insistent, signaling a fire drill. My little sister Ginny had graduated to a second floor class, and even though I sometimes let on to my friends that she was a pain, inside myself I really wanted to make sure that she got down the slide safe and sound.

Before the first clang of the bell had faded away, I was up and standing in front of the window. It helped that my desk was right next to it. Jay hustled into line and bumped into me. "Watch it," I said.

"Shush," said our teacher, Mr. Walters. "You should set an example for the younger students. If this were an actual crisis, they would need you to show them the way."

"Set an example," Jay whispered. I could hardly keep from laughing out loud. I let my chin drop but kept my lips together, pulling my face into a long and haughty expression.

Jay snorted and said, "If the teachers are gonna stand around and talk our ears off while we burn up, at least we'll die with dignity." Then Jay copied my expression.

Mr. Walters swept a glance around the room to make sure there were no stragglers. Then he gave me a nod. "All right, you may proceed."

The window was up and I was out. I slid down on the seat of my pants and sprang up with a flourish as soon as my feet touched dirt. Jay was right behind me. I turned and waited for the rest of my class to get down. I watched Polly, Rebecca Ann, and Melinda from my class swoosh toward me and Jay, holding their skirts tight against their legs and blushing when they caught my eye. I didn't smile back, though. I wanted to show them that I was a real man in any crisis, and not one to take escaping from a fake fire lightly.

When the girls neared the bottom, Jay jumped in front of them. He screamed and put up his hands as though afraid that they were going to knock him over. The girls shrieked, and Jay jumped aside at the last minute, grinning from ear to ear. He was so childish.

The smaller kids started trickling down the slide, and I

bumped Jay out of the way so I could be at the bottom for Ginny. I was well aware that the girls from my class were still milling around, watching me.

Ginny's friend Ted came into view, his feet looking half a size too big in his older brother's cast-off shoes. He started down the slide, raised his eyes, and caught sight of me. Instead of grinning, as I had expected him to do, his eyes went round as eggs, and his mouth opened up and let out a scream. He twisted over, his fingers scraping the smooth metal surface of the slide as though trying to climb back up.

"Ted!" I called. "What's the matter?"

"Get away!" he screamed in a voice of abject terror. "Mommy!"

I reached for him. Unbelievably, he screamed even louder. I managed to get ahold of him and set him on his feet. He took off, running blindly, until Polly caught him. She bent down to talk to him, and his arms wrapped around her neck as tight as a cockleburr on a sheep's hide.

I looked at Jay and spread my hands. "What did I do?"

Jay shrugged. "I dunno."

I looked up the slide just in time to see my little sister's face peer out of the window. She looked down at me, so I waved to her. "Come on, Ginny. I'll catch you."

Ginny's eyes sprang wide open, and she shook her head with such violence that I was worried it might come off. I could see her teacher lean out to speak to her, and after a moment, Ginny disappeared from view. What was going on?

Jay took my place at the bottom of the slide. Even though I'd been told to stay with my class during every fire drill, my concern for Ginny was stronger than the school rules. I walked around to the door where the first floor kids were trickling outside. I didn't go against the tide but waited and watched until Ginny appeared, clutching her teacher's hand.

I walked over and looked down at Ginny's tear-stained face. "Why didn't you slide down?" I asked. "I would have caught you."

Ginny let go of her teacher's hand and grabbed me around my waist. "Daniel, where were you?"

Was she blind? She'd looked right at me. "I was at the bottom of the slide. I told you to come down."

Ginny shook her head against my shirt. "That wasn't you. I heard you calling, but I couldn't see you anywhere."

I pushed Ginny away and stared down at her. "Then who was standing at the bottom of the slide, I'd like to know?"

Ginny's eyes went wide, and fresh tears welled up and spilled over her cheeks. "It was a scary old Indian with a mean face and long, black hair."

It felt like my heart stopped beating, and I had the awful sensation of spiders crawling down my neck. Was Ginny seeing things, or had something happened to me that I didn't even know about?

I pulled Ginny into a hug and held her until we both quit shaking.

Still, that wasn't the worst of it. The worst day was a stormy one, with the dark clouds hanging around after a night of thunder and lightning that kept waking me up. So it was with bleary eyes and dragging step that I made my way to school that morning.

I should have stayed home.

The inside of the school felt as cold and damp as the air outside, and even the marching music failed to lift my spirits. Maybe there was something wrong with me. Maybe I was coming down with a fever. I reached out and touched a finger to the radiator in the upstairs hallway. It was stone cold. Why hadn't the heat been turned on?

We found our seats in our classroom. Then Principal Erickson stuck his head in our door. "Boys and girls, I'm going downstairs to see what's taking Mr. Fjeldsted so long to get the heat going. Keep your coats on. We'll soon have the problem set to rights." Then he was gone.

That was the last time I ever saw him.

I shivered in my jacket and tried to follow what my teacher, Mr. Walters, was saying at the front of the room. I watched him scratch the chalk across the black surface of the board and I wrote down the spelling words five times each.

It seemed as though time had almost stopped, and that the day would never end. I felt as though I were trapped in a sticky fog that wouldn't let me move freely. Something was dragging at my heart and slowing down my whole world.

I was sure that enough time had passed that the school day should have been over when the door to our classroom banged open. We all looked up to see who would dare burst in without knocking first. I couldn't believe it when I saw Miss Jenkins standing inside the doorway, her face alive with panic. "There's a situation, Mister Walters. Please, will you come?"

I think that she was trying to be discreet, but her cryptic message only served to whet the appetite of our class. We looked at each other with wide eyes. Some of the girls looked worried and scared.

"Sit quietly and wait for further instructions," Mr. Walters barked. Then he was out the door at a run.

If he really thought we'd sit quietly, he didn't know us very well. Some of us crowded to the windows to see if we could see anything. Others peered out the door, shushing the rest of us in the hope that they might hear something that would give them a clue as to what was going on.

My earlier fatigue was replaced by a terrible anxiety. It was not an improvement.

It seemed to be another long day before Mr. Walters came back, his face creased with emotion. "Boys and girls," he said. "You are dismissed. Everyone go home."

He was met with shocked silence. This had never happened before—ever.

"Class, stand up," Mr. Walters said, his voice patient, as though speaking to a group of first graders.

We stood. I shivered inside my jacket, the cold of the room

taking on a sharp edge that cut through to my heart as sure as a north breeze could cut through my shirt in the dead of winter.

"Dismissed," Mr. Walters said. "Go straight home." Then Mr. Walters disappeared through the doorway without even waiting to make sure we followed orders.

We murmured among ourselves as we made our way to the door, leaving behind our books and papers and filing out into the hallway, boys on one side and girls on the other, heading for the exit.

My concern for Ginny overrode my training. I risked breaking ranks in order to detour to my sister's classroom and pick her up. I knew deep inside that something was terribly wrong, and I wasn't leaving my sister's safety to chance.

I found Ginny lining up with her class, her eyes wide with worry. I reached toward her, hoping that she would recognize me and not mistake me for some old, grizzled Indian. Ginny smiled up at me and took my hand. Her teacher was still shooing students from the corners of the classroom toward the line. When I lifted my hand, Ginny's teacher saw me. I pointed to Ginny and then to myself. The teacher nodded, and I took my sister with me.

Our exit from the school took us down the hall that held the stairway to the cellar. The cellar door was open, and Mrs. Wintch stood at the top of the stairs looking down, tears coursing down her cheeks and her mouth all twisted as though she were trying to hold in a scream.

I slowed my steps and looked over my shoulder. No one else was around. "Are you all right?" I asked.

Mrs. Wintch looked at me, but I don't think she really knew who I was, or else she wouldn't have said what she did. She may have mistaken me for someone older since I was tall for my age and was holding Ginny by the hand.

"Oh, they're dead, they're both dead!" she cried.

Her words struck me with a pain as sure as if she'd slapped my face. "Who?" I asked. I wasn't sure I really wanted to know. The question just popped out without me thinking about it.

"Mr. Fjeldsted and Principal Erickson! They're both dead!"

Mrs. Wintch wrung her hands and stared down the stairs, not even trying to wipe off the tears that rolled down her cheeks.

Mrs. Wintch was old. Surely she was confused. I had seen the principal alive not more than an hour ago. He couldn't be dead. She must be mistaken. But I didn't say any more. I just took Ginny home.

Later that day, Dad came in, his face as saggy as a half-full bag of potatoes. He gathered us together and told us that, as near as they could figure, Mr. Fjeldsted had gone down into the basement to check on the furnace and saw that the floor was underneath a couple of inches of water. He must have tried the light switch, but it didn't work. It seems that he waded through the water and turned on the light bulb with the pull cord that hung down beside it. Something was wrong with the wiring, and electricity coursed through him, killing him on the spot.

When the principal went down to check on Mr. Fjeldsted and saw him lying in the water, he'd rushed to help him. He must have tried the light too, because he was electrocuted as well.

When Miss Jenkins had gone looking for the principal, she spotted the two bodies in the dim light coming in from the basement windows. Miss Jenkins never left the safety of the stairs but ran back up and called on Mr. Walters for help. Mr. Walters knew enough to call the city electrician, who turned off the power before anyone went in to retrieve the bodies.

I never could walk down that hallway again. I always went around the long way. Even seeing that door from a distance sent a cold snake of fear sliding down my back.

The legend of old Washakorie's curse flared up. It was all the kids talked about, even after the school re-opened, which didn't happen until after the funerals.

"It's just like he said," Jay told me, his voice tight with excitement. "He said there'd be two dead men for the two skeletons that were dug up. It's just like he said."

I didn't answer him. There was nothing else to say.

The school bell was the pride of the whole community. Besides being used to summon us to school and for fire drills, it was rung for any and every important occasion. The Fourth of July was brought in with its clear tones ringing against the mountainsides and rolling back down into the valley. It was rung through the cold air of Christmas Eve and the bright morning of New Year's day. It sounded on election days and Founding Father's Day. The ring of the bell would herald every celebration in town.

After the deaths of Mr. Fjeldsted and Principal Erickson, that all changed.

The day after the funeral for the school custodian and principal, I woke up in the middle of the night with my heart pounding in fear. Then, with my eyes wide, and scared in the darkness of my room, I heard the unmistakable toll of the school bell ringing in the midnight air. The sound set my teeth on edge. Who was ringing that bell? There was no town meeting in the middle of the night, and it wasn't any holiday that I knew of. Could it be that someone's house was on fire?

I hopped out of bed and went to the window. I looked out and saw nothing but stars.

Suddenly feeling like a scared little boy, I hurried out into the hall and down the stairs to my parent's room. Their door opened before I even reached it, and my father stepped out.

"Daniel?" he said. "What's going on?"

"I don't know," I said, my voice squeaking on the last note, but I was too scared to feel embarrassed.

"I'll go see what it is," Dad said. "You stay here."

He didn't have to tell me twice.

Mama came out in her dressing gown. She sat me at the kitchen table and fixed me some homemade bread spread with a generous layer of plum jam. Normally I love plum jam, and my mother is hard pressed to keep it in the house. But tonight I could only nibble the edges of the bread. The ominous sound of the bell filled my ears and took away my appetite.

I gave up and set my bread and jam down on my plate. "Where's Ginny?"

"She must be asleep."

"How can she be?" I asked, getting up from my chair and heading for Ginny's room. I imagined her cowering in a corner of her room, her hands tight over her ears to try and shut out the gong of the night bell.

Mama followed me. I pulled open Ginny's door. Her still form made a hump under her blanket, and her golden head rested quietly on her pillow.

"See?" Mama said.

"I've got to check," I answered, moving into the room.

"Don't you dare wake her up," Mama warned.

"I won't," I whispered. I couldn't tell Mama that my heart was worried sick that Ginny wasn't sleeping at all but was really lying there dead.

I bent over Ginny and saw the slight rise and fall of the covers over her chest. The flood of relief that coursed through me was hot enough to bring tears to my eyes.

I backed out of the room and pulled the door shut. "How can she do that?" I asked as we headed back to the kitchen.

Mom shrugged. "I don't know. Maybe she's dreaming of bells."

As soon as I sat down at the table, the bell stopped. The silence that followed was as ominous as the ringing had been.

Dad came in a little while later. Mom and I both looked up at him. He shook his head. "No one was at the school."

Mom spoke up. "But who rang the bell?"

Dad spread his hands. "No one was there. I met Ed Winters and Theodore Southby at the door. Ed opened the school with his keys, and we all headed for the bell room. The rope was swinging up and down all right, but no one was in there." Dad dropped his hands and shook his head. "It was the darnedest thing. As we watched, the rope went limp and the bell quit ringing. We checked the whole building. It was empty."

There was silence. I looked from one parent to another. Neither one of them seemed to know what to say.

Finally, Mom broke the silence. Her quiet voice made me jump. "Lock the door, Harold. Let's all go back to bed."

I headed for my room but I didn't go in. When I heard my parent's door click shut, I went back to Ginny's room. I grabbed the extra blanket that Mom kept folded at the foot of her bed and curled up on the rug on her floor. I lay there and shivered for a long time until I fell into an uneasy slumber.

After that night, the bell would sometimes ring of its own accord. We couldn't figure out why until we made the connection that someone in town always died when the bell rang.

That wasn't even the worst of it. When World War II broke out and Donny Simms went out to fight in the war with some other fellows, the bell rang itself again. The odd thing was, no one in town turned up dead.

For a couple of days, it seemed as if the spirits that cursed the school were way off track. Then Donny's mom got a telegram telling her that Donny had been killed in battle two days earlier.

I got to hate that sound of the ringing bell. It sounded for a couple of other dead soldiers until the end of the war silenced it. I had a hard time going to school under the cold, metal eye of that haunted bell. It seemed to be watching me like a vulture, waiting for the day when it could ring itself over my cold, dead corpse.

One good thing that happened at school was the arrival of our new film projector. We were awfully proud of it, even though it only showed black and white films instead of the new colored movies that were in theaters.

Unfortunately, we didn't get to see any wild west films, but what did we expect for free? We were treated to the life cycles of bugs, forest fires, and cultures from other countries.

The projector was kept under lock and key by Mr. Madsen,

who served as our school librarian. He was the only one qualified to operate it, and was ultimately responsible for its safety.

Usually on film days we couldn't keep quiet. We'd only seen a couple of them when we were informed one day that we'd be watching a film on East Africa. I was excited to see it, as I didn't imagine that I'd ever get to Africa in my lifetime. Mr. Madsen threaded the film through the projector and switched it on.

"All right, everybody, quiet down now," he called. I couldn't really see much point in that, since the films were silent.

"Turn off the lights," Mr. Madsen called. Someone flicked off the light, and the black and white images burst into life on the screen. After a few minutes, we were all silent, mesmerized by the unfolding scenes of life in Africa.

Then something odd happened. A reddish tinge spread from behind a grass hut on the right side of the screen. It crept out toward the black natives dancing up and down with their spears held aloft. The film image switched to a row of giant bugs skewered on a long stick held over a fire. The reddish stain was there too. After a few seconds, the redness crept back into the corner of the screen and disappeared.

I glanced back at Mr. Madsen, who was fiddling with the controls. He looked back up at the screen and gave a quick nod.

I leaned over to Jay, who was sitting beside me. "Did you see that?"

"Yeah. Creepy."

From the other whispers going around the room, I knew that everyone had seen the red stain.

That wasn't the last time. From then on, a reddish tinge would creep across the different films we watched every once in a while, and not always from the same place. The day I really started dreading films was when shadowy, indistinct faces superimposed themselves over the images on the film.

One day, Mr. Madsen asked me to carry a stack of paper supplies for him. I said I would. I filled my arms with paper and followed him up to his supply room. I watched him put his key in the lock. I heard it click when the bolt disengaged, and I followed him in. There was the unmistakable whir of machinery, and I fixed my eyes on the film projector. It was turning its little wheels in a race to nowhere. The film posts were empty.

I shot a sideways look at Mr. Madsen, wondering if he was embarrassed to be caught in his carelessness of leaving the projector on.

Mr. Madsen turned to stare at me. "Do you see that?"

It seemed to be a pointless question, but I answered, "Um, yes, sir."

"I did not leave that running. I know I didn't. Who else could have a key to this room?"

I didn't answer. Mr. Madsen didn't really expect me to. He was just talking to himself. I set the paper down on the counter and got out of there as fast as I could.

The next film we saw was on the Grand Canyon. A kid named Arlo Anderson was goofing off at the front of the room, braying like a donkey when a string of pack mules appeared on the screen. Mr. Madsen's warnings to be quiet didn't have much effect, since the girls were giggling in delight at Arlo's antics.

At last Mr. Madsen abandoned his post beside the projector and headed toward the front of the room. I expected to see Mr. Madsen grab Arlo by the ear and pull him out into the hall. Then Arlo would be braying for real.

Before Mr. Madsen reached Arlo, the projector clicked, then clunked, then whirred. A hush fell over the room when the film began running backwards. My eyes were drawn from Arlo back to the screen. Donkeys scurried up the Grand Canyon trail backwards as fast as they could go, their tails uphill of their heads.

"Mr. Madsen," I said, my voice sounding small in the darkened room. I raised my hand as though waiting to be called on, even though Mr. Madsen wasn't looking at me. I could see from the flickering light bouncing off the white screen that Mr. Madsen's eyes were fixed on the projector. I turned and looked too. No one was even within arm's reach of the machine that busily churned the film backward as though it had a mind of its own.

From then on, I always sat at the back of the room, on

whichever chair was closest to the door. I would avert my eyes when the red tinges appeared and disappeared. I fought down panic when strange and shadowy images popped up on the screen that had nothing to do with the film subject. Before long, Mr. Madsen returned the projector to the manufacturer as defective.

As one of the upperclassmen, I was privileged to claim membership in the fearless group called "Ledge Monkeys." It was our good fortune that the school was built with six-inch wide ledges all the way around, just underneath the windows. In spite of the fact that they were out of reach from the ground, we found a way to overcome that obstacle. Jay was the first one to dare climbing up the fire escape slide in order to gain access to the ledges that circled the ground floor windows. He was an insufferable braggart after he completed his circuit without falling to the ground. Of course, we other fellows couldn't let him get away with a solo victory, so we all followed suit. When we were caught, we were scolded and told not to walk the ledges anymore.

In spite of the warning, it was only a matter of time before we set our sights on the more challenging second story ledge. Because we'd been warned by school authorities to keep off, we made our second story attempt under cover of dusk. This took more courage. Still, I was willing. After all, I was nearing eighteen and almost ready to graduate. I had to leave some sort of legacy behind.

We climbed up the fire escape, pulling with our hands and pressing our bare feet into the bottom corners at either side of the smooth, metal slide. When we reached the second story, we climbed out onto the six-inch ledge, our hands gripping the rock that lined the window openings so hard that the grit dug into our fingers. It was a harrowing journey, much higher than it appeared to be when looking up from ground level. Making the trip at dusk added an element of danger, and I almost wished I'd stayed home. Almost.

When we completed our circuit, I felt like a king. I whooped and let go of my death grip on the building, sliding my way down the fire escape to the ground. I was invincible.

It seemed to me that we'd achieved the ultimate accomplishment, since a fall from the second story would almost assuredly result in a broken limb or two. But the next thing we knew, Arlo had his sights set on the third story window ledge. When the rest of us expressed our doubts, Arlo called us a bunch of broody hens.

"But what if you fall?" Jay said. "At that height you risk more than a broken bone. Death is more like it."

"That's why I'm gonna do it," Arlo bragged.

"We wouldn't be much help to you if we were all standing up on that ledge." Jay looked around at us other guys. "We'll follow along underneath to catch you."

Arlo was silent for a moment. "Ha!" he said. "What makes you think I'll fall?" But it was all bluster on his part, and he agreed to Jay's plan.

Arlo looked very small in the moonlight, perched up there at the top of the fire escape, twenty-six feet in the air. I could only imagine how he felt when he looked down at us.

Arlo reached out from the fire escape and grabbed the edge of the window frame in slow motion. He positioned his feet on the ledge. I stared up at his heels hanging out over the ledge. Only his toes held him on. One slip, and we'd have to catch him or watch him die.

I glanced around at the other fellows gripping the edges of a blanket that we intended to use to catch Arlo if he did happen to fall. I hoped that we'd all head in the same direction if worse came to worse, instead of pulling each other off balance. I shivered at the thought of the ghostly bell-ringer pulling the rope for Arlo.

Arlo began shuffling around the window ledge. We followed along underneath him, keeping our hands tight on the blanket and our faces pointed upward. The other fellows were washed pale with moonlight. It made them look like a gathering of ghosts staring up into eternity. I wondered if they were as scared as I was.

Arlo rounded the first corner. Now that the fire escape was out of sight, he moved with more caution along the second wall. His progress was painfully slow. When he neared the end, I noticed that I was getting a crick in my neck, but I didn't dare look away. We were Arlo's only hope if things went wrong.

Arlo rounded the second corner and I relaxed my grip a little. It looked like he was going to make it. His face was pressed pretty close to the windows as he passed his hands from one window frame to another, his feet shuffling along in increments of inches. He neared the third corner and pulled himself over to the next to last window. He froze. I could see his back go rigid. Then a scream of sheer terror ripped from his throat, the most frightening scream I'd ever heard come out of a human being. My disbelief turned to horror as I watched him let go. He tipped backward, and I stood staring with my mouth gaping open. A tug on the blanket nearly pulled me over.

"Move it!" Jay yelled. I blinked and stared in dismay at the obstacle before us. We'd never be able to save Arlo's life now. A big, blue spruce tree grew right where we needed to stand in order to catch him. Panic seized me and I screamed.

Arlo hit the spruce branches and crashed on through. Since his single, awful scream, he'd made no sound. I wondered if he was dead. Could the curse have claimed a third victim?

The other fellows yanked on the blanket, and I followed them to the edge of the spruce. With no help from me, they managed to get the blanket stretched tight just as Arlo rolled out of the bottom branches. By some miracle, he landed on our makeshift trampoline, but we weren't prepared for his weight. We all grunted and tumbled to the ground, ending up in a tangle of arms and legs.

My voice quavered. "Is he dead?

The only answer was the wild scrabbling of Arlo's arms and legs. As soon as his two feet touched earth, he was gone, racing across the lawn faster than I'd ever seen a person run before. If he was bleeding, I didn't see it. If he had a broken bone or two, they weren't slowing him down any.

We all scrambled to our feet and hurried across the grass after him, figures running in the moonlight. We found him huddled in a ditch.

"Arlo?" I asked, afraid that the fall had somehow damaged his brain. "Are you all right?" Maybe he'd hit his head and didn't know us anymore.

Arlo's eyes were as big and white as two moons, looking past me toward the upper story of the school. "Horrible," he muttered. "Watching me." He shuddered and covered his face with his hands. "Something's up there."

We helped Arlo home, casting glances over our shoulders at the dark building watching us go. The school windows glowed an eerie silver in the moonlight. When I had to part company with the fellows and head for my own house, I admit that I ran all the way.

The next day, we discovered that someone had pushed the dressmaking class's full-length mirror up against the corner window, right at the spot where Arlo had been so spooked that he took a dive off a third-story window ledge. It was no comfort. For all we knew, the Indian ghosts pushed it there after we left the school.

Eventually, I graduated and moved away. It was several years later when I heard that the school was being torn down. My curiosity got the better of me, and I made the trip to my old hometown. I almost didn't recognize the place. Part of the grand old building was reduced to a pile of rubble. I noticed that several people were picking up bricks and carrying them off as souvenirs. As soon as I wondered if I should take one, I decided not to. There were still ten years left of the Indian's curse.

This story is based on reports that Chief Washakorie warned the settlers of Spring City in the late 1800s that they shouldn't build a school on top of a Indian burial ground. They built the school anyway, and an angry Washakorie cursed the school.

Several decades later, two men were electrocuted in the basement of the school after flooding rains. There were also reports of students seeing the faces of old Indians on the upper-classmen who were stationed at the bottom of the fire escape slides, haunting music sounding from a piano where no one sat, and strange images and reddish tinges coming and going on the screen where a projector showed various educational films. One student walking the third-floor ledge screamed in panic and fell through the branches of an evergreen tree. He told his friends that he'd seen an old, spooky Indian face looking out at him from the upper window. The next day, the boys discovered a full-length mirror pushed up against the glass at the point where the boy had fallen.

Source: *Book of Mt. Pleasant 1938; Hansen Family History 1976.*

So Scared

"Bringing in the sheaves, bringing in the sheaves," I sang along with the other kids as I bent to grab another handful of wheat stalks. I knew all the words of the old hymn by heart, and it was fun to belt them out as I worked. Mary Ann Hyde always made our work go faster when she had us sing as we gathered up the loose stems of grain that had escaped harvesting.

I pretended that I sang only because Sister Hyde asked me to, but truth be told, sometimes I'd sing when I was out herding the cattle, after looking around to make sure that no one was within earshot. I didn't always mind having anyone hear me sing, but lately my voice would catch me off guard, warbling up to a squeak before it dropped back down to where it belonged in its new, lower range. Since I had a couple of older brothers, I knew that being thirteen would do that to a guy, but no one said I had to like it.

I carried my armload of wheat over to the wagon and saw my mother headed toward it with a small bundle of wheat stalks gripped in her hands. She wasn't looking at me, though. Her head swiveled from side to side, her brow wearing a familiar crease of worry that had been there for so long that she even looked worried in her sleep.

I knew that Ma was scared spitless of the Indians. Even if she hadn't told me over and over again, I would have seen it in her eyes. She was like a mouse in constant fear of meeting up with a cat. Her graying hair was even the color of a mouse's fur.

I glanced over at Sister Hyde, who was laughing at something Iona Clay had just said. Even though Sister Hyde was about the same age as Mama, her brow was smooth, and the lines on her face were laugh lines. Even though she'd lost every single baby she'd ever had, she still found joy in life.

Why couldn't Mama be like that? Why couldn't she stop being afraid? The mountains were dotted with cheerful spots of autumn red and yellow, and the bugs were less voracious since the cold nights were nipping them to death and the days were only warm enough for a few lazy flies to bumble along through the air. There was a lot to be happy about.

When I dropped my wheat in the back of the wagon, I caught a whiff of the fried chicken and corn bread that sat under the fabric covering the lunch basket. Dared I snitch a mouthful? No one would need to know. I could chew and swallow pretty fast. It was almost time to eat lunch anyway. I rationalized that I'd just take less food when it was finally passed around.

I glanced up to see if anyone was watching. Mama's eyes connected with mine, and the opportunity was lost. I gave her an innocent smile. She tried to smile back, but her eyes didn't look the least bit happy. Sister Hyde had somehow talked Mama into coming along to help glean the fields today, even though Mama preferred to stay in the cabin with the latch solidly in place, carding wool and spinning and baking. She wouldn't generally open the door for anyone unless Pa was there. She had been told, along with everyone else, to give food to the Indians when they came asking for it, but Mama didn't like to. She trembled at the very thought, and if she was alone, she'd usually pretend she wasn't home.

Ever since she'd started on the trek across the plains, Mama had been deathly afraid of being killed by Indians. She was still afraid, even though we'd lived in Spring City for several years. Poor Mama. There was more to life than being afraid.

I turned away from the wagon. Strains of "Johnny's So Long At the Fair" drifted along the staggered row of children moving down the field together, bending and picking up wheat stalks as they went.

A movement caught my eye, and I turned to see three riders approaching. I gave a sudden start and stared hard, not wanting to believe my eyes. Indians were coming.

My first thought was to find my mother. I looked for her where I'd last seen her, but she wasn't there. If she saw the Indians, she'd be in a terrible state. In near panic, I glanced all around me but didn't see her anywhere. "Mama?"

The sound of muffled sobs reached my ears. I bent over and saw my mother huddled under the wagon, her head bent down and her hands covering her ears. She'd already seen the Indians. I decided that she was in the best place she could be.

I hurried down the row of gleaners. "Sister Hyde," I said. "Indians."

The children close enough to hear me stopped singing and whirled around to see for themselves. Sister Hyde turned to look too, her blue eyes watching the Indians approach. They were close enough that I could see a tomahawk in the lead rider's hand. Their heads bristled with feathers, making them look like birds of prey swooping down to pluck up some small animals for their bloody supper.

"Keep singing, children," Sister Hyde said.

If I didn't sing, I might scream. "He promised to bring me a bunch of blue ribbons," I sang, too scared to be embarrassed when my voice cracked on the word "blue."

"Orson," Sister Hyde said, putting her hand on my shoulder. "Go over to the wagon and get the food basket."

I suddenly remembered when Charles Christensen told me about the time he was just ten years old and his grandma filled a cloth sack with cookies for him and his little brother Fred, to eat on their way home. They headed off across the hills instead of sticking to the road. Charles insisted on rationing their sweet treat to make it last.

But Charles completely lost his appetite as soon as he heard the thud of horses' hooves. His worst fears were realized when a couple of Indians rode up to the brothers on their horses, shaking their fists and calling out things he couldn't understand. The Indians looked at each other and laughed, and then shook their bows and knives at the boys. Charles knew they were done for.

One of the Indians pointed to the sack that Charles clutched in his hand. Charles was so afraid that he couldn't even move, but Fred wasn't. He grabbed the sack away from his older brother and thrust it up at the Indian. The Indian slid down from off his horse. Charles was so scared that he almost peed his pants, but Fred stood his ground. Charles was sure that he would be forced to watch the Indian grab Fred and ride off with him.

Instead, the Indian grabbed the bag, opened it up, and looked inside. Then he gave a mighty whoop and leapt up onto his horse. He took off at a gallop, and his partner sheathed his knife and wheeled his horse in hot pursuit.

Charles wasted no time in grabbing Fred's hand and hightailing it home. After that, he always stuck to the road.

I turned away from Sister Hyde and made a dash for the wagon, passing the row of gleaners whose eyes were fastened on the Indians who would soon be within scalping distance. Sister Hyde's voice rang out over the field with the words to "Johnny's So Long At the Fair:"

"Oh, dear, what can the matter be? Oh, dear . . ."

The other children gradually began singing along with Sister Hyde as I sprinted toward our lunch. I heard Mama whimpering underneath the wagon when I grabbed the basket. "Stay quiet," I said. Then I turned and headed back. No Indian would get my Mama today if I had anything to do about it. They'd have to kill me first.

Sister Hyde walked toward the Indians, who brandished their weapons and bared their teeth. They could strike her down as easily as not, yet she didn't hesitate. She walked straight and tall, though she was no taller than me, and raised her hand, palm out flat, in a gesture of peace.

My feet slowed. I knew I needed to take the food to Sister Hyde, but she was just too darn close to the Indians for my liking. Yet I had to do whatever I could to help the others, especially Mama.

I set my jaw and headed for Sister Hyde, singing, "Johnny's so long at the fair." The food in my arms didn't even tempt me any more. My stomach was too twisted in knots. If I had snitched a bite earlier, it would have been wasted because I knew the fear in my belly would have thrown it up by now.

The three Indians turned their eyes on me—eyes so black that I felt as if I were staring into a well that had no bottom. "He promised to bring me a bunch of blue ribbons," I sang, my voice cracking on "ribbons."

One of the Indians grinned wickedly. He turned and said something to the others before he sang a quavering note in a falsetto voice that sounded eerie and wild. They all burst into laughter. My face burned with embarrassment, but I kept on singing. The Indian with the tomahawk pointed to the basket that I held.

Sister Hyde gestured from the basket to the riders and spread her arms out with her palms facing backward. She glanced over her shoulder at the children and shook her head, and then stared at the Indians. "If I give you food, you leave." She pointed in the direction the Indians had come from.

I moved beside Sister Hyde, still warbling about Johnny at the fair. The children's voices were so soft I felt as though I was singing a solo. Still, I sang, my voice off-key and cracking. If we were lucky, my awful singing would give those Indians a bad headache.

"Thank you, Orson." Sister Hyde lifted the basket. The Indian with the tomahawk leaned down and grabbed it in his large hand, the muscles on his biceps bulging as he raised the basket up to his lap. He lifted the lid, and his face split into a grin. With a quick shout, he wheeled his horse and rode away. His two companions took off after him, yelling and whooping.

Then my legs gave out and I sank to the ground. I didn't mean to, but it just happened.

"Orson? Are you all right?"

"Yeah. My legs just stopped working." I pushed myself back up onto my feet. "I've got to see to Mama."

"Why don't you take her home, Orson?"

"She won't go."

"Why not?"

"Because the Indians are out there." I felt a quiver in my stomach even as I spoke the words. I was scared too.

"Well, without something to eat, we really can't do much more today," Sister Hyde said. "Let's all go home."

She rounded up the children and I walked over to the wagon and bent down to see my mother curled up, rocking and crying softly.

"Mama, they're gone," I said, putting my arm around her as best I could. "The Indians have gone."

Mama kept her hands over her face. "I'm so scared," she said. "I don't want to be killed by Indians, I don't! Someday they're going to get me, I just know it."

"They're gone," I said again. "You're okay."

Mama wouldn't come out until Sister Hyde led the children over. "Everyone put your gleanings in the wagon," she said, her voice lilting and cheerful. "My, but we got a lot done this morning. Come on, everyone, back to town, and we'll see if we can't find some bread and honey for our lunch."

The sound of Sister Hyde's voice gave Mama the courage to crawl out from under the wagon. She crept close beside it all the way home, shooting frequent glances at the mountains through her red-rimmed eyes.

Mama would never go gleaning after that.

It was only a couple of weeks later when I went out herding cows so they could forage one last time before we'd have to shelter them for the winter and feed them on stored hay. Papa was away working at the shingle mill. The shingle cutter that he'd brought over from England made the work go much faster, and the shingles he made with it were more uniform than the ones made using the old method. He always had more than enough work to do. Papa's skills were in high demand with all the people moving into the valley, and he wasn't home very often. Mama had never liked being left alone, but she liked it even less now. Even though my older brothers were all moved out and on their own, and I was the last one living at home, I couldn't stay with

Mama. I had to see to the cows.

"Look, Mama, if any Indians come around, they'll only be wanting a little food."

Mama gripped her hands together and looked as though she might start crying right there on the spot.

"Okay, Mama, I'll keep in sight of the house. I'll hurry down if I see anyone coming, all right?"

Mama nodded her head. "I'm sorry I'm so scared," she said, biting her bottom lip.

"It's okay, Mama. Sometimes I get scared too."

Mama sank into her rocking chair and took up some mending with trembling hands. I cut myself a thick slice of the bread that Mama had baked several days earlier. It was dry and hard—really only good for bread and milk. Even though John had moved out months ago, Mama still baked as though all my brothers were still home.

I hurried outside, welcoming the freedom of being outdoors. I soon had the cows moving up into the little draw above our homestead.

The sun was lowering in the sky when I noticed a horse headed for the house. At first I thought Pa was home early from work. When I looked closer, I saw that it wasn't Pa at all but an Indian brave. I knew that I would never get to the house in time to intercept him, but I took off running anyway. I saw the Indian dismount and disappear around the corner that hid the front door.

I'd raced a few hundred yards when Mama's scream brought me up short. Her wail of terror sliced through the air and cut deep into my heart.

I stared at the house as my heart fought to escape my chest. What should I do? I knew in an instant that I couldn't handle this alone. I had to get help.

I turned and ran for the sawmill and Pa. When I got there, it felt like my lungs were ready to explode. I grabbed at the stitch in my side that had me bent sideways. "Pa," I gasped. "An Indian . . . Ma."

Pa didn't wait to hear any more. He ran out to his horse, jumped on, and helped me scramble up behind him. I hung onto Pa's waist as we raced for home.

The Indian's horse was gone. We dropped to the ground and dashed inside.

Ma was curled up on the floor, retching; the floor beneath her head was stained with blood. "Emmeline!" Pa gasped. He bent down and touched Ma's hair. The blood was oozing out of Ma's mouth, and she had her arms folded tight around her middle.

"Orson, go fetch the doctor, and if you can't find the doctor, get Sister Hyde."

I spun around and dashed out to the horse, my eyes blurred with tears. Why had I been such a coward? Why didn't I keep running to the house to save Mama from the Indian? The sight of Ma curled up in pain spurred me to ride faster than I'd ever ridden before. I got the doctor and, for good measure, Sister Hyde too. But I was too late. Mama died anyway.

"It's not your fault, son," Pa said, blinking back tears.

"I didn't keep going to help her after I heard her scream," I said. "I got scared. I should have kept going, but I was too scared."

Pa was shaking his head. "It's not your fault. I don't know how the Indian got inside in the first place. Maybe she forgot to latch the door."

The doctor said it looked as if she got hit in the stomach once, hard enough to break something up inside. Pa clamped his jaw shut and wiped his eyes. "With that bread we found on the floor, we can only guess that the Indian didn't like the old, dry bread your mother gave him. In his anger, he must have kicked her to do so much damage, and she was hurt too badly for the doc to do anything. And if the doc couldn't do anything, neither could you. She would have gone anyway, son, so none of this is your fault."

In spite of Pa's reassurance, it was still hard to convince myself.

While digging Ma's grave at the edge of the cemetery, we

struck a solid rock ledge, so we shifted the hole over to one side. Pa said we wouldn't mark the grave until after the Indian unrest died down.

When I was an old man, they built a wall around the cemetery, using the rock ledge we'd uncovered while digging Ma's grave as a foundation. Ma's grave was on the outside of the wall, so my poor mother, scared to be alone for so much of her life, was consigned to a solitary resting place in death.

Orson Hyde and his wife Mary Ann Price Hyde never had any surviving babies of their own, but Mary Ann enjoyed children and took them with her to glean the fields around Spring City, Utah. They would sing as they picked up the stalks of grain that had escaped harvesting.

One day in the 1860s, three warriors carrying tomahawks and bristling with feathers rode up to them. Mary Ann told the children to keep singing. She gave the Indians all their food. Appeased, the warriors left the group unmolested.

Source: *Saga of the Sanpitch*, 6: 17.

Glenn and Terri Morris told me the story of Glenn's great-great-grandmother Emmeline Arundale, who married John Lee in 1829 in England. When they immigrated to Utah, Emmeline could not shake her fear of being attacked by Indians. In 1866 thirteen-year-old Orson Pratt Lee saw an Indian enter their cabin and heard his mother scream. When Orson fetched his father, they found Emmeline on the floor, coughing up blood. After she died from her injuries, they buried her in an inconspicuous grave beside a submerged rock ledge. When the cemetery walls were erected in 1925, they enclosed the opposite side of the ledge, missing Emmeline's grave entirely. The pioneer lady who was so consumed by fear in her mortal life now rests in a lonely grave, alone outside the cemetery wall.

Around 1871, Charles John Christensen and his brother Fred were sharing a bag of cookies from their grandmother as they walked home from her house. Suddenly, some Indians swooped down on horseback, taunting the boys and laughing. The brothers finally surrendered their sack of cookies, and the Indians rode back into the hills, leaving them alone.

Source: *Saga of the Sanpitch* 6 (1974): 17; 21 (1989): 45.

Guess Again

I folded a dish towel four times over before opening the oven door. A wave of hot air hit me and forced me to turn my head. I grabbed the bread pans and plunked them onto the sideboard. Then I closed the oven and fanned my face.

Even though the kitchen door was open, it was still awfully hot. The open door let the bugs in, but having a few of them flying around was better than melting into the floorboards. I didn't want to melt. I wanted to go riding. Even though I'd done a full day's work, I was never too tired to ride.

I glanced around the house. The dishes were done, even though the grease from the family's breakfast of side pork had been awfully hard to clean from the plates. I'd already refilled the hot water reservoir on the back of the stove. It was hissing and sputtering in its metal confines, but it would quiet when the fire died down.

After the Seely family had left for town this morning, I'd fed and watered the calves and hogs, scattered grain for the chickens, mixed the dough, baked the bread, swept the floor, washed up the dishes, and finished the mending and darning.

Now I grabbed the hard bar of homemade soap and shaved some into the pan that sat on the back of the stove. In no time, the soap shavings would be softened and ready for the next batch of dishes or laundry or for scrubbing the outhouse seat.

I hurried out the open door and scooped up an armload of firewood, noticing that it would be time to split more soon. I had to fetch another armload to fill the box right up to the top. I chipped a corner off the salt block and dropped it into a bowl of water. I'd use the salted water for the family's morning mush.

Now all that remained was the afternoon milking of the cow.

I really liked working for the Seely's. They paid me a generous thirty-five cents a week plus my room and board. The best thing about working for them was the privilege of riding their horses after my chores were finished.

I grabbed the milk bucket and headed for the barn, glad that I had refused the Seely's offer of a ride into town with them. If I'd gone, I would have had to catch up on my work when we got back, and there wouldn't be any time for riding. But now, I could get in a good, long ride before dark.

As I squeezed the milk into the bucket, I imagined galloping across the fields, my hair loose and streaming out behind me. I loved riding; I loved the freedom and the sense that I was flying across the fields. The only bad thing about it was when the Indian boys spotted me, they'd come galloping up behind, whooping and hollering until they caught up to me. They'd ride along beside me, calling out things that I didn't usually understand, but it was easy to guess that they were teasing me. I did my best to ignore them, but still, I hoped that they wouldn't see me today.

I finished with the milking and headed back to the house—one arm out to the side to balance while my other arm hung down heavy with the full milk bucket. I carried the milk down into the cooling cellar and strained it through a cloth. I skimmed the cream from the morning milk pans and poured it into the butter churn. Then I put the morning's milk into a pitcher. Next I carried the milk pans upstairs, washed them, and took them back down so I could pour the newly strained milk into them. I set the bucket at the bottom of the steps.

I looked at the butter churn out of the corner of my eye. I knew it was full enough to churn a batch of butter, but I wanted to ride. But what if the Seely's came home before I got back? I couldn't bear to think of them being disappointed in me.

I sighed and walked over to the churn. I worked the cream until the butter formed. The basement no longer felt cool; I was warm from the effort of churning the butter.

I scooped the butter out of the thick buttermilk and slapped it into the butter molds. I should strain the rest of the buttermilk, and pour it into a pitcher, but daylight was burning. I was hot, I was impatient, and I figured that I could save one chore for when I got back from riding.

I picked up the dirty milk bucket and made my way upstairs. As hot as the cooling cellar had felt, the kitchen was still hotter. I longed all the more for the breeze that would cool my face when I rode the horse out across the fields in the early evening air.

I used a ladle full of water from the soft, soapy pan at the stove's back to scrub the milk from the bucket. I knew from experience that it was easier to clean when the milk was fresh then after it had time to dry. I carried the bucket into the yard and rinsed it with clean water from the pump until it shone. Then I carried it back in the house and turned it upside down on the drain board.

Finally. I was ready.

A long shadow stretched across the floor and slanted across my feet. Alarmed, I whirled around. An Indian man stood in the doorway. The gnarled, old fist of one hand grasped a bent and battered bucket. His other hand clutched a heavy walking stick. He stared at me with one scarred eye, puckered up in a dark face criss-crossed by deep age lines. I sucked in my breath and stared at him with growing horror. I knew this Indian, and I was scared to death to be alone with him.

I'd seen this man walking along the back roads, supporting himself on his heavy walking stick. Brother Seely had warned me that this particular Indian wasn't quite right in the head. I believed him. More than once, I'd watched him swing that very same stick at young Indian girls who surrounded him and teased him. With his face twisted in fury, he would swing the hammer-like knob on top of his stick at the girls' heads. They would squeal and dance out of the way. I knew in my heart that he would not hesitate to smack one of them with the full force of his strength if he got the chance.

"Bizhi nehwe." I jumped at the sound of the Indian's voice.

His mouth barely moved, and his eyebrows were pulled down. My stomach turned over. What had he said? I was fairly certain that if I didn't figure it out, there would be dire consequences.

The Indian raised the bucket in his hand and held it out toward me. The last thing I wanted to do was to get any closer to him, but if I didn't take the bucket, it might be the end of me. I took a few steps and stretched out my hand to grab the bucket handle. He let go.

I glanced into the bucket. It was in much worse shape up close. Someone must have thrown it out. Dirt clung to the dents that riddled the sides, and bits of grass and insect parts rattled around the bottom.

I wrinkled up my nose. Then I noticed that the Indian was staring at me. What did he want? Was I supposed to clean out his bucket? He could have rinsed it himself in the stream, but maybe he considered it women's work. I grabbed a cloth and wiped the inside clean. Then I turned it upside down over the floor. I would worry about sweeping up the dirt and bugs later.

I looked up at the Indian. He twisted his head slightly so that he could see me better out of his puckered eye, but he didn't make a move to take the bucket from me. A shiver ran down my back.

He must be looking for food. Bread was the most obvious choice, since I'd just baked some, and the smell was heavy in the air. I plucked a loaf from off of the drain-board and dropped it into the bucket. Then I held it out toward him.

The Indian didn't touch the bucket but reached inside and pulled out the bread. He tucked it under one arm. He gestured to the bucket and said, "Bizhi nehwe."

My heart sank. "Bizhi nehwe" obviously did not mean "bread." What else could it be? Then I had an idea. Since he'd gone to the trouble to bring me a bucket, it must be something liquid that he was after. He could have scooped all the water he wanted out of the stream, so he must want milk.

My heart lifted. There was plenty of milk in the cooling cellar. Once I fetched him some, he would surely leave.

"Just a minute," I said, holding up my index finger as though that single gesture would make him understand my words. I turned and made my way across the floor to the cellar door. Then I walked down the narrow stairs. I set the bucket on the floor and poured some of the morning's milk into it. I picked up the bucket and turned to go. As soon as I saw the Indian standing at the bottom of the steps, blocking my only exit, the room shrank in around me and I gasped. He had descended on his moccassined feet so quietly that I hadn't known he was there.

I gathered my wits in time to keep from dropping the milk, but I couldn't keep my hand from shaking when I held the bucket out toward him.

He clamped his walking stick under one arm along with his bread, and took the bucket in both hands. Instead of turning around and climbing out of the cellar to set me free, he tipped the bucket up to his mouth. When he tasted the milk, he lowered the bucket so fast that milk splashed over the sides.

"Dechende!" He up-ended the bucket and spilled the milk out onto the dirt floor.

I was outraged. That milk had taken a lot of my precious time to get, and he was wasting it.

"Stop that!" I demanded, my hands on my hips. I glared at the Indian.

He thrust the battered bucket toward me again. "Bizhi nehwe." His puckered eye glittered, and he pulled his walking stick out from under his arm and clutched it in his gnarled hand.

I decided not to argue any further. I snatched the bucket out of his hand and turned to survey the cellar. What else could he possibly want? My eyes landed on the cream that had risen to the top of the milk pans. That must be it. I pulled my ladle across the pans several times over and dumped the cream into the Indian's bucket. Then I whirled around and shoved the bucket at him.

His good eye narrowed with suspicion before he lifted the bucket and tasted what was in it. He yanked the bucket away from his mouth and glared at me.

"Bizhi nehwe!" he shouted. Little flecks of cream spewed

from his lips. He tossed the cream onto the ground and threw the bucket at me. I flung my arm up just in time to deflect it. It clattered to the floor, and the Indian gripped the head of his walking stick. He stared at me with his jaw thrust forward and his brows pulled down.

I stared back at him, breathing heavily. What else could he want? We had no whisky—no firewater. The flutterings of panic pushed away my anger, and I bent to retrieve the bucket. I had to get out of here. Maybe I could tell him that "bizhi nehwe" was upstairs, and then when I got there, I could run out of the house and escape.

I turned away from the Indian again, my mind working desperately. The back of my neck tingled with cold chills when I realized that if he got angry enough to take a swing at me with his stick, I wouldn't have anywhere to run.

My eyes flitted from the milk pans to the cream bowl to the milk pitcher to the butter molds. What could he be after?

Then my desperate eyes landed on the butter churn where the buttermilk waited patiently to be strained. Buttermilk! It was my last hope.

I dropped the bucket onto the ground, grabbed the butter churn, and tipped it over the bucket. The lumpy buttermilk splashed inside. I snatched the battered bucket and pushed it at the Indian. He wasted no time in tipping it up to his mouth.

There was nothing else for me to offer him. My eyes darted to the stairs. Could I push my way past him as he tasted this final offering and make my dash for freedom? With fear nipping at my heels, I didn't worry that I could outrun him, but would he be quick enough to grab me if I tried to squeeze past? Or would he hit me with his stick before I could get out of reach?

The Indian lowered the bucket and raised his hand to wipe the buttermilk from his lip. It was too late to run. He grunted. Then he turned and mounted the stairs on silent feet.

I nearly collapsed with relief. I'd finally guessed right.

I made myself wait until the stairwell was clear before I finally put a foot on the bottom step. When I reached the top, I slowed and peered around the doorjamb to see if the Indian was still lurking in the house. He was nowhere in sight.

I hurried to the door and looked out. The Indian was moving away, tipping the bucket up to his mouth every so often to take a swig of buttermilk.

I slammed the door and lowered the bar across it. Then I let myself shiver and shake a bit before I washed out the butter churn.

I wouldn't be riding today, or the next time the Seely's went into town, either. The next time they went shopping, I'd be going too.

In 1882, the Indians were less threatening to settlers than during the Black Hawk War but could still dish out a world of hurt if angered. Bothilda Hansen was a girl of sixteen, working at the Moroni "Rone" Seely house in Indianola when she was visited by an Indian man who was known for his strange ways. Bothilda had seen him threaten Indian girls who teased him by swinging his heavy walking stick at them. The Indian carried a bucket to Bothilda but spoke no English, so Bothilda had to guess what he wanted until she got it right.

Source: *Saga of the Sanpitch* 6 (1974): 48; 12 (1980): 105; 17 (1985): 98.

Bizhe newhe: butter milk
Deschende: not good

Indian Court

"But, Chief, you said that we should bring our problems to you and you'd take care of them," Little Dog said, turning his head so that he was looking at me from the sides of his eyes. I knew this evasive gesture. As sheriff, I'd dealt with Indians for quite some time.

It had been fifty years since Black Hawk signed the peace treaty, and the Indians and whites were pretty well used to each other by now. We'd had enough time to condition the Indians to our way of justice—the white man's method of holding a trial and using a jury to decide a person's guilt or innocence. The Indian's tradition was one of swift justice. If someone did wrong to you, then you did the same to them, or worse, as soon as possible.

"Little Dog, I've got to have evidence before I can take it to court."

"Isn't my dead brother enough evidence for you?" Little Dog said in a voice so soft that I could barely make out his words.

"I'm sorry," I said, and I meant it. "Your brother was a good man. It's just that I have to have some evidence of who killed him."

"It was Alchesay," Little Dog said, speaking the name of a tribesman who'd had brushes with the law before. "He's been jealous of Bear ever since he bought his own flock."

Bear had been a diligent sheep man, learning the trade while working as a herder for white men over the course of several years. Bear was an ambitious fellow, with a proud bearing and a quick mind. He saw that the new sheep industry was bringing in good returns for his white neighbors, so he worked and saved and bought himself a few sheep that he soon built into a small, yet prosperous flock.

Bear had been the one to dub his brother Little Dog, since he'd followed the older Bear around like a puppy. Little Dog had been known as Little Dog for so long that I don't think he even remembered his real name. I sure didn't.

Bear was known by some Indians and whites alike as Joe Standing Bear, but to Little Dog he was always Bear.

"When I find the evidence, I'll put Alchesay in jail," I said.

Little Dog gave me another sideways look before he turned and walked out of the door. I felt sorry for him, but there was nothing else I could do, so I went back to my paperwork.

The next day I was called out to Martin Begley's farm to look into some vandalism that had been done to his tractor. I spent some time questioning Martin before his wife called him into the house. I poked around looking for clues until Martin's son Henry came back from town.

"What'cha doing sheriff?"

"Someone came in the night and dented your dad's tractor. I'm checking into who might have done it. Did you hear anything last night?"

Henry Begley's ears turned red, and he ducked his head.

"Well, Sheriff, I'm afraid that it was me."

"You?"

"Yes, sir. I was going to tell Pa, I just didn't find the right time yet."

"Why didn't he know about this when it happened?"

Even though he wasn't quite a man, Henry stood as tall as me. "Well, maybe that's because I came out after he was gone to bed."

"What were you doing working in the dark?"

"Well, you know this is a new tractor, and Pa's been doing all the driving. I wanted to take it for a turn around the field myself. I figured that I'd get to drive it lots sooner if I just helped myself instead of waiting for him to say I could."

I raised my eyebrows at Henry, but it was he who spoke.

"Yeah, I know. I'll probably never get to drive it now."

With the problem resolved, I headed back to my office. I was only about a mile out of the Begley's place, riding easy, when I spotted Alchesay on the side of the road, a cloth sack hanging heavy from one of his hands. When he looked up and saw me, he gave a guilty start. He clutched the sack to his chest, turned away, climbed a fence, and trotted off through a field.

"Alchesay!" He didn't look back but picked up his pace. I knew he'd heard me, and wondered if I should chase him down. I decided not to, but I'd be sure to talk to him about this later.

The next day I rode out past the Indian village and saw about a dozen men sitting in a circle. Little Dog was one of them. I got off my horse and walked over to them. All conversation ceased, and most of them ducked their heads to stare at their hands in their laps.

"Hey, how ya doing?"

No one answered me.

"You having a powwow?"

"Just talking," Little Dog said.

"About what?"

"Indian business."

I looked around at all the bowed heads. "Anything I can help with?" I asked.

"No," Little Dog said.

Something felt wrong here. I looked around at the gathering again, but no one would meet my eyes. There wasn't anything I could do about it. They weren't breaking any laws, as far as I could see.

"Anyone know where I might find Alchesay?" I asked.

A couple of heads turned to look at the others, but it was Little Dog who answered me. "No."

I waited a few more minutes. No one said anything, so I cleared my throat. "Well, call me if you need me," I said.

"Okay."

Silence.

I turned and walked back to my horse. It wasn't until I

mounted and headed out that I glanced back and saw several of the Indians raise their heads to watch me leave.

Later that day, I spotted Alchesay crossing the street in front of the tobacco store.

"Hey, Alchesay," I called. He darted a look at me and he tensed, as though he might start running.

"Alchesay," I shouted again. "I need to talk to you."

His shoulders slumped, and I knew he'd stay put. When I got close to him, I smelled whiskey. If he'd been drinking, I may not get much information. On the other hand, the alcohol might loosen his tongue. I figured it was worth a try.

"Alchesay, I called out to you yesterday and you ran away from me."

"I didn't hear," he mumbled.

"I think you did."

Alchesay was silent.

"What was in the bag you carried?" I asked.

Alchesay shuffled his feet. I wasn't sure he was going to answer me, but I was determined to wait. At length, he said, "Feathers."

I was taken aback. "Feathers?"

Alchesay nodded.

"What did you want feathers for?"

Alchesay did not raise his head. "Fletching arrows."

It was a reasonable answer, since the Indians fastened feathers on their arrows in order to balance their flight through the air. Still, Alchesay was being evasive. I knew it, but without evidence that he was guilty of anything besides carrying around a sack full of feathers, I couldn't arrest him.

"Next time you hear me calling, you stop. Understand?"

Alchesay nodded.

"If you don't, I'll put you in jail," I said.

Alchesay nodded again.

I turned and walked away. When I glanced behind me, Alchesay was gone.

It was later that same day that I got a report from Jeb Thomson that widow Marks was missing some hens. She'd been home alone and hadn't been able to get word out until Jeb rode by to check on her. He brought the report straight to me.

"She doesn't think it was a fox," Jeb said. "It looked like someone lifted the latch and snuck off with them."

Alchesay, I thought. He'd been moving away from Widow Marks' place when I saw him with the bag. It could just be a coincidence, but my gut instinct told me otherwise. Feathers. Ha. Feathers with chickens still attached was more like it.

"Okay, Jeb, thanks. I've got an idea of who to talk to about this."

Well, even if Alchesay might be getting away with murder, at least I could catch him for stealing chickens.

I stood up and got ready to go out to Alchesay's place when Mr. McCreedy came in pulling young Clem Fife by the arm, hollering about his broken window. Clem's mother was right behind them, crying her eyes out.

I couldn't just leave them like that, so we worked out the problem. Clem agreed to help Mr. McCreedy with some of his chores in order to pay for the broken glass.

By then it was supper time, and I went home to eat. There'd be time to deal with Alchesay in the morning.

The next day, I swung up on my horse and headed for the Indian village. I stopped the first Indian I saw and addressed him from the saddle of my horse. "Where's Alchesay?"

He shook his head but didn't speak. I rode a little further and saw two Indian women sitting in front of a house. "Have you seen Alchesay?" One woman looked at me with wide eyes full of shocked surprise. The other answered, "No," and tugged at the silent woman's skirt.

"You sure?" I asked.

"Yes." The women bent their heads over the buckskin they held spread across their laps.

Something was awfully strange. I slid down from my horse and walked him to the next yard. A familiar figure ducked around a corner of the house. "Little Dog?" I called. "Is that you?"

Little Dog came back into view with his back straight, but his eyes fixed on my horse instead of me.

"It's me."

"Have you seen Alchesay?"

Little Dog's eyes shifted up to my face and then darted away. "No," he said.

Something was wrong here, but I couldn't figure out what it was. I knew from experience that asking more questions at this point would get me nowhere. Alchesay was a flighty character, no question about that, but still, where else would he be if not here? Well, no matter. He was bound to show up sometime.

"If you see him, let me know. I need to ask him some questions."

Little Dog gave me a single nod. He flashed a glance up at me, and I caught a glimmer of knowing in his eyes. He knew something that he wasn't telling me. Even if I were to haul him in and lock him up—even if I were to resort to primitive torture—I sensed that he would never tell me his secret.

I headed back to my office, my mind puzzling over the look in Little Dog's eyes. I tried to make sense of it, and played over the past few days in my mind. He'd come to me looking for justice for his brother. I'd said it could take some time to get evidence, if there was even any to get, and it was plain that he'd been disappointed.

Then there was that meeting I'd interrupted a couple of days back, the meeting of a dozen braves sitting on the ground in a circle, with other Indians looking on. Why weren't all of them in the circle? That was the natural order of things, unless they were having a powwow inside a tepee. Then they would only include those who needed to be there.

A dozen. There was something significant in that, I was sure of it, but the meaning escaped me.

I thought back to Alchesay running with a sack full of feathers, which must have been stolen chickens or I'd swallow my own boot. I'd seen Alchesay just the day before. He couldn't have gone far.

I reached the sheriff's office and took care of my horse, before stepping inside. Jeb Thompson was waiting for me.

"Sheriff, I got that list of men you wanted, the ones for the jury."

I stopped, my heart pounding hard against my ribs. I suddenly remembered why the number twelve was so significant. There were twelve men on a jury.

I never saw Alchesay again.

An Indian was murdered by another Indian in the early 1900s. Since the white men did nothing about it, an Indian council convened and voted on who they believed the guilty man to be. A few days later, the man named as guilty disappeared and was never heard of again.

Source: *Saga of the Sanpitch* 28 (1996): 41.

FROM LITTLE THINGS

Christine pulled another paper off the stack at her elbow and centered it on the table in front of her. She tried to decipher the blotchy scrawls that wormed across the page, but she was too tired to make any sense of it. She pushed the paper aside and stood up, placing her hands upside down on the small of her back to stretch out the kinks.

There was no better job in the world than that of schoolmistress, but sometimes it was hard. When she had students who struggled with their work, she felt their frustration. She imagined that for some of the younger children, learning the alphabet was like her trying to learn the Indian language. She'd never been able to make sense of their syllables, and wondered if she ever would.

There was time enough for papers later. Right now she just wanted to go to bed.

Before she reached the bedroom where her husband was already sleeping, Christine heard a knock on her door. It startled her, but she wasn't surprised. She often had callers at odd hours, because she had done some doctoring in the settlement and was said to have "the touch."

Now her interest in who was here and what the problem was chased her fatigue away. She moved to the door and pulled it open. She gasped at what she saw and took a step back.

The huge Indian brave at her door followed her in, seeming to take her retreat as an invitation to enter. Christine stared at the man, hoping he wasn't to be her patient. Then she noticed a small bundle clasped in the giant's arms. The little Indian baby was such a small thing, and it was so quiet. Its little mouth was open and it struggled to breathe. From the sheen of sweat on its small forehead, Christine guessed that the child was suffering from fever.

Without a second thought, Christine held her hands out toward the sick baby. The Indian handed him to her, and said something in his own tongue that Christine could not understand.

"Yes, he's got a fever," she said, even though she doubted that the Indian understood her.

Christine took the baby and pulled a tablecloth off the shelf. She tossed the tablecloth on the table without unfolding it and laid the baby on it. She looked inside the little mouth, and felt the baby's head. "Oh, you are so sick," she crooned to the infant, who lay silently sweating and staring up with big, black eyes. His innocence and obvious misery tugged at Christine's heart.

"Him sick. Make well," the Indian said.

Christine guessed that the boy had been suffering for some time, since he seemed to have lost his will to even cry. He merely lay there, struggling for air, waiting for the end to come with a patience that was far beyond his years.

Christine turned to the stove and slid some wood inside, checking the teakettle to make sure that it had water in it. Steam could help the baby breathe easier, but she needed to do something for his fever. She tried an alcohol rub, which made the little boy gasp and the whites of his eyes show all around the dark irises. He trembled and shook. Christine wrapped him up again and held him close, carrying him over to the now steaming teakettle. She lifted the kettle off of the stove and carried it back to the table.

"Bring me a bowl," she said, pointing to the cupboard. The Indian strode over to the cupboard, picked up a bowl, and brought it back to Christine. Then he folded his arms and watched as Christine poured hot water into the bowl and made a makeshift tent with another tablecloth. As she worked, she spoke to the baby in soft tones, murmuring reassurances that he would be fine, that he shouldn't worry, and that she would do her best to take care of him.

Christine grabbed a handful of dried poplar bark and dropped it into the bowl of boiling hot water.

In spite of the steam tent, the baby's breathing became shallower.

"No, little one, hang on," Christine said.

The baby closed his big, dark eyes.

Christine turned to the big Indian and looked up at him through eyes wet with tears. "Your baby is very sick. I am afraid that he will die."

Christine tensed as the Indian stared at the child, and then back at her. He looked again at the baby, and lifted his chin toward his son, as though telling her to get back to work.

"Him sick," he said.

Christine wished that she had some beef kidney; even if she did, she sensed that there wasn't time to heat it and tie it to the boy's feet in order to draw the fever out. It was simply too late.

Christine dipped a cloth in cool water, squeezed it out, and wiped the baby's sweating brow with it. The boy sighed, and was still.

Christine stared down at the dark little body. Tears escaped her eyes and slid down her cheeks. She hadn't even known this boy two hours ago, yet the time she'd just spent trying to make him well had nestled him into her heart. Now her chest squeezed with pain at the loss of this little spirit.

A brown arm reached past Christine and scooped up the boy as though he were a rag doll. Christine whipped around, her eyes blazing through her tears. "You treat him with respect."

The Indian stared at her through his dark inscrutable eyes but didn't answer. He turned and carried his son out the door and disappeared into the darkness.

Only after they were gone did Christine have the sense to realize that she should have been scared. Yet the Indian had not taken his frustration at the death of his son out on her. At least, he hadn't yet. He might come back later to settle the score.

But Christine didn't think so.

Weary in spirit and body, Christine crawled into bed beside her husband.

Two weeks later, the news of an Indian killed several miles south reached the settlement. It was rumored that the Indians were on the warpath and out for revenge. Even though Christine hadn't seen the Indian father since he'd left her house, she wondered if he, too, held revenge in his heart. She listened with growing trepidation to the reports of the whites who were killed. After several battles that took lives from both sides, the whites and Indians settled into an uneasy truce.

One evening when she was home alone, Christine heard a knock on her door. "Who's there?" she asked.

"Open door." The deep command could only have come from an Indian.

Christine shrank back. "What do you want?"

The Indian spoke again, but through the solid wooden door, his words made no sense to Christine. Then there was a heavy silence. At last, the voice said, "Him sick, make well."

Christine's heart all but stopped. Was the baby's father back for revenge?

The Indian spoke again. "Open door."

There was something so compelling in the voice that Christine moved toward the door. She stared at it, her heart tripping over a little burst of fear. The latchstring was out.

She realized that the Indian could have pulled on the latchstring and let himself in at any time. This small detail reassured her, and Christine pulled the door open.

The big Indian stood there, much as he had on their first meeting, but she almost didn't recognize him. His face was painted and he carried a bow in one hand. Her heart faltered.

"We come," the Indian said, walking his fingers through the air. "You no fear. You no sick." He formed his arms in a protective circle in front of his body, and shifted the quiver of arrows on his shoulder. Christine flinched. The Indian shook his bow at her. "I watch, you stay well," he said.

Christine was confused. The Indian must have seen it on her face, because he said again, slowly and distinctly, "You well."

He turned and left. Christine shut the door and pulled the

latchstring inside. Then she sat and stared at the door, waiting for her husband to get home.

It wasn't until the next day that Christine learned that there had been a raid on the settlement. Livestock were stolen, and some of the men who'd gone out intent on saving the animals had been shot. Lee Johnson's barn was burned to the ground, and the Dunbars lost all their poultry after the Indians killed their dog.

Christine hurried out to help the wounded. When she applied a poultice to Stan Severne's wounded leg, her brow creased with worry, hoping against hope that the treatment could save the leg from amputation.

Stan looked up at her and said, "Who's your Injun friend?"

Christine's startled eyes flew to Stan's face. "What?"

"Yer Injun friend. After I took that arrow, I laid there on the ground for the longest time, pretending I was dead so they wouldn't kill me for real. I saw him standing in front of yer house, bow and arrow ready, waving his fellows on past yer place if they got too close. How'd you get your own Injun guard?"

Christine didn't tell him. Her heart swelled so big with gratitude that it was difficult to speak. The Indian knew that she'd tried to help his baby, not kill him. She was glad that he had understood her intentions, and she felt relief in knowing that she had a big, strong Indian ally.

Mrs. John McAllister tells this story based on her grandmother's life. Around the 1850s, Christine did her best to save the life of an Indian baby but wasn't able to. The baby's father took the baby away from her house without a word.

Later, when the Indians attacked the settlement, the baby's father stood guard over Christine's house and wouldn't let any harm come to her.

Source: *Saga of the Sanpitch* 2 (1970): 35.

Index

About the Author

Shirley Bahlmann grew up among different ethnic groups in New Jersey, but she didn't have any experience with Native Americans until she was named honorary "Princess Roan Eagle" of the Sioux tribe. After her family moved, she was fascinated to find Native American placement students in her new school, and she even struck up a friendship with Loretta Nez, who taught her a few Navajo words.

Shirley prefers the country smells of horse and cow manure to the city aromas of gas fumes and fast food. She lives in rural Utah with her husband, Bob. They are the parents of six sons—Andy, Jeff, Scott, Zackary, Brian, and Michael—the three youngest of whom still live at home. She's delighted to have two daughters-in-law, Heidi and Jamie, and two grandchildren, Marcus and Anneke.

Odd People: Andapu Oyate is the fifth of Shirley's *Odd* series, following *Against All Odds, Isn't That Odd?, Even Love Is Odd,* and *Unseen Odds.* She is currently laughing her way through several funny pioneer stories to see if she has enough for a volume of humorous pioneer tales.

Read excerpts from these books and check out what else she's up to on www.shirleybahlmann.com.

0 26575 78359 9